The Status of Women
in Preindustrial Societies

The Status of Women in Preindustrial Societies

Martin King Whyte

PRINCETON UNIVERSITY PRESS

PRINCETON, NEW JERSEY

To Ronnie

Contents

List of Tables

Acknowledgments

WHEN a piece of research takes much longer to complete than its initiator foresees, it is perhaps axiomatic that the list of acknowledgments will grow in length. More than five years were spent working on this particular piece of research, and I cannot hope to adequately thank here all of those who were involved or provided encouragement. What follows represents an abbreviated summary of the many debts of gratitude I incurred.

My interest in cross-cultural research was first stimulated through a seminar I took from John Whiting and David McClelland as a graduate student at Harvard University. Further stimulation came through exposure to the Comparative Sociology Program directed by Paul Hollander and Donald Warwick and work on comparative family systems under Ezra Vogel at the same institution. The opportunity to teach a course on comparative family organization here at the University of Michigan led me to realize the need for a systematic cross-cultural study of the status of women in preindustrial societies.

The funding for the data collection stage came from two sources: first, a Small Grant from the National Institute of Mental Health and, when those funds ran out, a faculty research fellowship from the Rackham Graduate School of the University of Michigan. Computer funds and student trainees were provided by the Department of Sociology at the same institution. Two sociology graduate students played special roles in this research. Kristin Moore worked with me at the inception stage, helping me to review the literature and draft the cross-cultural coding form and participating in the pretest. Kris provided many ideas and insights that

I incorporated in the study and stimulated my own thinking through the somewhat different perspective she brought to these matters. Patricia Paul worked with me later, participating in both the cross-cultural coding and the computer analysis. Her willingness to stay on in spite of other obligations in order to help me tie up the loose ends while I was on leave conducting new research in Hong Kong proved invaluable to the completion of the research.

The coding itself took longer than anticipated, and before we were done seventeen coders had been involved, including Patti and myself. The others were Jane Barrett, Fran Berge, Louise Berndt, Leila al-Imad, Tirbani Jagdeo, Amy Jorrisch, William Jungers, Jocelyn Linnekin, Julie McNeil, Judith Peters, Eileen Reinhardt, Joel Riff, Gayle Saini, Jean Samson, and Robert Thaler. The social science backgrounds and foreign language skills these coders brought to the project helped the laborious coding process go relatively smoothly. Donna Beuerle helped smooth out my many difficulties in managing research funds. Technical help and advice were provided by Dan Ayres, John Fox, Tom Wilkinson, and Colin Loftin. All of the secretaries in the Michigan sociology department were involved in typing one or another of the several drafts of the manuscript, and they performed this task admirably and efficiently. A variety of friends and acquaintances read the manuscript at some stage and provided useful advice, criticism, and encouragement. I would like to express particular thanks to Patricia Paul, John Ware, Karen Mason, Beatrice and John Whiting, Jennie Farley, Anne Foner, Gilbert Rozman, and Kathleen and William Whyte. I bear sole responsibility, of course, for the final product.

My greatest debt is to my wife, Ronnie, to whom this book is dedicated. She provided vital emotional support and encouragement throughout the ups and downs of the research and writing, and she maintained her interest and good cheer in spite of being subjected to my reading of several versions of each chapter as the manuscript was revised. All of those mentioned, but especially Ronnie, share in the credit for this book having survived its rather difficult gestation period.

Martin King Whyte
Ann Arbor
March 1977

The Status of Women
in Preindustrial Societies

CHAPTER I

Introduction

WITH the upsurge of the women's liberation movement and the rising interest in ethology and the animal origins of humanity, the public has been bombarded with scholarly and not-so-scholarly studies of the status and role of women in America and in other societies, and explanations of how things got to be the way they are. It is with this question of origins that the present study is primarily concerned. We will be considering the issue raised in the debate about how the position of women relative to men has varied and changed over the course of human evolution. As yet the debate on these issues has led to very little consensus. The passions surrounding the struggle to change the lot of women have led many writers to substitute polemic and unquestioned assumption for open inquiry. The literature in question is filled with generalizations that are extremely dubious and sometimes blatantly false. On many issues, quite contrary positions can be found in this literature. We hear from one authority that in low-technology tribal societies, "Insofar as work is divided and leisure is possible, women appear to work longer and at more menial tasks [than men]" (Collins, 1971, p. 9). On the other hand Margaret Mead (1949, p. 190) states, "The home shared by a man or men and female partners, into which men bring the food and women prepare it, is the basic common picture the world over." Both of these generalizations can easily be challenged.

Not only do writers disagree about what the role of women relative to men is around the world, but also about the reasons for whatever patterns do exist. Some authorities present a picture of male domination of women stemming from the evolutionary adaptations of early humans to a way of

3

life based on hunting and warfare, with the genetically imprinted male dominance continuing to shape the relations between the sexes today (Tiger, 1969). Others see a period in early evolution when matriarchy and the rule of women throughout social life existed, a period that gave rise to a universal mutiny of men and their subjugation of women, a subjugation that is still with us today (Bachofen, 1861; Engels, 1902; Davis, 1971). Some have seen the forces of industrialism and other forms of modernization producing improvements in the lot of women relative to men (Collins, 1971), while others have seen in these same forces the further degradation of women (Boserup, 1970).

Some of these disagreements stem from semantic and conceptual differences; from the different ways various authors think about the status and role of the sexes and what indicates high or low status. Yet in the heat of the argument, a number of very basic preliminary questions often go unexplored: How much does the status of women relative to men actually vary from culture to culture and from society to society? How does the status of women in one area of social life—e.g., religious, political, economic, domestic, or sexual—relate to their status in the other areas? What forces and institutions cause women to have higher status in one society than in another? The anthropologist Evans-Pritchard noted in a lecture in the mid-1950s that the kind of systematic comparative work on the position of women that would be needed to answer questions such as these had not been undertaken, and suggested that this was due to both lack of interest and to the laborious effort it would take to conduct such a study (Evans-Pritchard, 1965, p. 40). Almost two decades later interest in the topic has revived, and new ideas and arguments fill the air, but it is still true that no systematic comparative study has addressed these very basic questions. (For some partial approaches, see Sacks, 1971; Schlegel, 1972; Zelman, 1974; Friedel, 1975.) In the pages to follow we report the results of a comprehensive cross-cultural research project designed to provide some answers to the

4

questions of how the status of women varies around the world and why it varies. By *cross*-cultural we mean that the data used come from ethnographic studies of many different preindustrial cultures, rather than from surveys and statistics gathered in industrialized societies. The *world* we refer to is thus limited to the social forms that existed prior to the advent of industrialized nation-states. For this reason our research has more to say about the origins and evolution of women's roles than about, say, whether women today are doing better in Russia or in America. Yet with this limitation in mind we can address a broad range of issues, and our sample is not restricted to the small, preliterate cultures that in less self-conscious times used to be called "primitive." Both preliterate hunting bands and communities in settled agrarian empires are included. Roughly speaking, out of our total sample of 93 cultures, about a third are nomadic hunting and gathering cultures, another third are peasant communities within complex agrarian civilizations, while the remainder are cultures intermediate in scale and technological development (e.g., tribal groups subsisting on herding and/or shifting agriculture). This variety allows us to consider how a wide range of *preindustrial* social forms are related to the position of women. Further information on the composition of our sample is given in appendix 4. The distinctive features of cross-cultural data are discussed in chapter II, while the possibilities and problems of generalizing from our findings to the situation of women in more complex societies are discussed in chapter VII.

Before we begin presenting our research results, we should examine some of the kinds of problems in earlier works that have led to both polemical heat and simple confusion. Some works treat the subordination of women either as a societal universal or as a universal since the days of some hypothesized primordial revolt of men against their previous women masters. One problem with such arguments is that if a pattern is truly universal, then explaining its origins or reasons for existence becomes difficult. One cannot easily test the validity of different explanations of a phenomenon unless that phenomenon varies in the societies under study. To explain the origins of such a universal pattern, one is reduced to speculating about events before the dawn of recorded history (as in Tiger, 1969, and Morgan, 1972) or referring to other universals (such as the aggression-related hormones in males used in Goldberg, 1973). However, as long as a pattern is universal these explanations rest mainly on plausibility, rather than on rigorous testing, and in this day and age one man's plausibility is often another man's (or woman's) incredulity.

Theories of universal patterns suffer from other basic problems. They tend to deflect attention from the very real variation in the role and status of women existing in various societies and cultures. For example, it is true that we know of no society in which women have been dominant over men in political life generally, i.e., there have never been any true matriarchies (Gough, 1972, p. 115; Goldberg, 1973; Bamberger, 1974). This is certainly an important fact, and one that merits attention and explanation, if only of the "plausible" type. Yet at the same time there are some societies in which women are completely excluded from all political posts and affairs, while in others they are eligible for some posts and have an important voice in certain political realms. Surely this latter variation is just as worthy of notice and explanation, particularly since such explanations will be more susceptible to empirical testing. We will see that when we look beyond the universals we can find many such important variations from culture to culture in the status and role of women, and it is these variations that are the focus of this study.

Another problem in the existing writings is that certain indicators are chosen to represent the general status of women, while in fact they may have no such meaning. The early studies by Bachofen (1861), Morgan (1877), Engels (1902), and others tended to note kin groups in primitive societies based on relationships traced through women (matrilineal

6

descent), myths in which women played a prominent role, and certain female-oriented peculiarities in kinship terminology. These features led them to posit a general stage of "matriarchy" in the evolution of humanity. Later scholars have demolished both the notion that there is a universal evolutionary sequence (say, from societies with matrilineal descent to patrilineal descent), and that women in societies with matrilineal descent have a particularly lofty status (Ronhaar, 1931; Hobhouse, 1924, pp. 159-160; Bardis, 1963). Hobhouse summarizes the argument about the effects of descent on the status of women, "What is really common among simpler peoples is not matriarchy, but mother-right [matrilineal descent], and along with mother-right, and where it most flourishes, it is perfectly possible for the position of women to be as low as the greatest misogynist could desire. . . . The woman is not necessarily any better off because she is ruled by a brother in place of a husband" (op. cit.; see also Lowie, 1920, pp. 189-191; Murdock, 1949, pp. 184-187). We will return later in this study to a discussion of the importance of descent for the status of women, but it should be clear here that there is no available evidence to suggest that matrilineal descent, or myths dealing with powerful women, or female gods indicate a present or past period of female supremacy.[1] Nonetheless, some uncritical contemporary writers continue to build theories of original female supremacy

1. Why matrilineal descent and matrilocal postmarital residence are followed in some cultures and not others has been the subject of some debate among anthropologists. Some research emphasizes that agriculture based on digging sticks or hoes, a division of labor where women do much of the work, and the absence of intercommunity warfare make possible an emphasis on the ties among related women. (In regard to the last factor, for the dispersed males in a matrilocal society, intercommunity warfare would often pit father against son and brother against brother.) See Aberle, 1961; Steward, 1955; Ember and Ember, 1971. In this study we will use the terms *matrilocal* and *patrilocal* to refer to residence with the bride's parents and the groom's parents, respectively. Other studies use the terms *uxorilocal* and *virilocal* to refer to the same thing.

on fragmentary information about selected aspects of the role of women in some early societies. For instance, Davis (1971) posits female dominance in the recently excavated Anatolian city of Catal Huyuk (see Mellaart, 1967) on the basis of a few such traits: the importance of women in agriculture, the existence of female goddesses, and the larger number of female than male skeletons found in gravesites. She goes on to construct a revived version of Bachofen's "gynocracy" (i.e., matriarchy) based on such evidence, without stopping to ask about the importance of men in hunting and warfare, the nature of sexual regulations, the division of household authority, and the type of political structure that governed the ancient city. By being very selective in the indicators used for the status of women almost any point can be proved, but we do not move any closer to real understanding.

It is not only the theorists of universal patterns who make the error of using limited aspects of the role of women as indicators of their general status. Young and Bacdayan (1965) were interested in explaining the variation in the status of women from society to society, as we are. They picked as their indicators the kinds of restrictions placed on women during menstruation. As they state in their article (p. 230), "surely the most obvious interpretation of menstrual taboos is that they are institutionalized ways in which males in primitive society discriminate against females" (see also Paige, 1973, p. 46; Millet, 1969, p. 47; Zelman, 1974). This interpretation, while perhaps the most obvious, may be incorrect. Other scholars have argued that menstrual taboos are symbols of the high power and status of women (Devereux, 1950), and a recent study presents empirical evidence for matrilineal societies showing that menstrual restrictions have no relation to patterns of male domination of women or the reverse (Schlegel, 1972, pp. 89-90). Clearly in the midst of such disagreement it is ridiculous to settle on menstrual taboos or any other single indicator as representing the general status of women relative to men.

In fact a number of earlier scholars have been interested

not in universals but in variation in the status of women, and they have used not one or two, but several aspects of the status of women. Yet none of these earlier studies is completely satisfactory for our purposes. Some of the earlier cross-cultural surveys took this approach (Hobhouse, Wheeler, and Ginsberg, 1915; Simmons, 1945), but they suffer from problems of poor samples, sources of varying quality, and vague coding criteria. Recent studies have sometimes looked more precisely at a wide variety of aspects of the status of women, but only for a limited selection of cultures or types of societies (Ronhaar, 1931, especially chapter 15; Schlegel, 1972; Sacks, 1971; Friedl, 1975). In some cases interesting hypotheses about the status of women and how it varies come from case studies of a single society (e.g., Brown, 1970), but these are not tested for other societies. In other studies scholars have done broad cross-cultural surveys restricted to particular traits that may or may not have relevance to the general status of women (e.g., Brown, 1963, for female initiation ceremonies; Heath, 1958, and Brown, 1963, for women's contribution to subsistence; Barry, Bacon, and Child, 1957, for the differential socialization of boys and girls). All of these studies help us more than the theorists of universals in that they seriously address the question of variation from society to society and present ideas and hypotheses for explaining that variation. Taken together, they provide useful guides that have helped us design our general cross-cultural investigation of the status of women.

The first guide is that we should work with a world cross-cultural sample of societies of many types. Only in this way can we feel confident that our findings will have some general validity, and only in this way will we obtain enough cultures to submit hypotheses to empirical tests. These considerations led us to use a cross-cultural world sample of 93 cultures. The nature of our sample and the strengths and weaknesses of the cross-cultural approach are explained in some detail in chapter II. Specific details on how the study was conducted from conceptualization through sample se-

9

lection to data collection and analysis are presented in appendix 1.

The second lesson we derived from consulting earlier studies is that we should be eclectic in our theoretical approach. There are so many different explanations of the status of women floating around today, most of which have never been subjected to empirical testing, that it seemed unwise to pick only a few for proof or disproof. Our approach instead has been to search for all types of explanations of variation in the status of women, no matter where they could be found. Our final list of hypotheses is presented in chapter III. There the reader will note that we have included hypotheses stemming from structural, Marxist, psychoanalytic, ethological, and other approaches, and in several cases the existing literature leads us to pose mutually contradictory hypotheses.

The third guide we drew from previous research is that we should be equally eclectic in finding measures of what we are trying to explain: the status of women. It has been noted (see Goldberg, 1973, pp. 68-69) that the term *status of women* is a vague one, a term by which one person may mean the rights of women, another the respect women receive, and others still different things. While in many studies this vagueness constitutes a problem, we deliberately selected this term because of its imprecision. We use it as a broad and inclusive term that may cover the differential power, prestige, rights, privileges, and importance of women relative to men. In collecting information about our 93 cultures we wanted to include items dealing with the status of women (thus broadly defined) in religious, political, economic, domestic, sexual, and other realms. In the end, after elimination of some items for reliability problems and the combination of some other items into scales, we were left with 52 different variables, all representing, perhaps, different aspects of this vague concept, the status of women relative to men. While it can always be argued that certain indicators have been left out, still the variables we ended up with cover a broad range of social life, broader than in any previous study. In chapter

IV we present the final 52 items on the status of women and show just how equally or unequally they are distributed across our 93 cultures.

We start with a wide range of hypotheses meant to explain why the status of women relative to men[2] is high in some societies and low in others, as well as a long list of indicators of the status of women itself. Before the two can be brought together we must do some preliminary analysis. We want to know whether, in fact, there is a general phenomenon we can call the status of women that has some sort of regularity cross-culturally. If such a general phenomenon exists, we can expect to find a pattern of statistical associations among a fairly large number of our 52 status items. If this is the case then we can combine these items into a single scale representing the status of women, and use this single scale to test our hypotheses. Yet possibly the status of women is a more complex phenomenon. Perhaps, for example, knowing that women have limited property rights or are subjected to severe sexual restrictions in a particular society will tell us little or nothing about their role in food production or their ability to participate in religious ceremonials. In this case we may find not a single general scale, but instead several discrete scales representing more narrow aspects of the status of women—such as their property rights and the restrictions on their sexual lives. If we have several scales representing different aspects of the status of women, we will have to test our hypotheses against each. We may find that a particular hypothesis is confirmed for a scale of women's role in production, but contradicted for a scale of their power and influence within the home. The first step, in any case, is an examination of the pattern of association among our 52 status items, to see whether one or more scales emerge. This step is described in chapter V.

2. Throughout this study when we refer to the status of women and other similar concepts we always mean "relative to men." However, for ease in exposition we will generally omit this phrase from now on, and the reader should bear in mind that it is always implied.

11

Once we have determined, in chapters IV and V, how the status of women varies around the world, we must then turn to the second major question: why it varies. In chapter VI the hypotheses presented in chapter III will be examined, using the scale or scales of the status of women that emerge in chapter V. It is at this point that we sift through and evaluate the validity of the theories and explanations of the status of women that have been put forward in recent years. In chapter VII we present our conclusions and speculate on implications our findings may have for other issues in the debate on the changing role of women. The study itself is followed by four appendices presenting additional information about our research. Appendix 1 covers the methodology used and the problems confronted. Appendix 2 lists the 93 cultures included in our sample. Appendix 3 lists the variables used in this study and the reliability with which they were coded. Appendix 4 uses selected variables to describe the nature of our 93-culture sample, particularly the representation within it of both simple and complex cultures.

Our goal is an ambitious one: to examine in a general cross-cultural study how a wide range of aspects of the status of women relative to men varies, and then try to explain why the status of women is higher in some societies and lower in others. Before we present our findings we must explain what the cross-cultural method is, and what it can and cannot do.

CHAPTER II

The Cross-Cultural Method

IN THIS study we attempt to get at the how and why of variation in the status of women by using a cross-cultural survey. This kind of survey involves coding for the presence or absence, or type, or degree, of various cultural traits over a world sample of cultures. In order to put our eventual findings in perspective, it is important for the reader to be aware of the peculiarities and strengths and weaknesses of this type of research. The first point to note deals with the terms *society* and *culture*. While we sometimes will use the term *society* in talking about the peoples included in this study, the sampling is actually based upon units called *cultures*, groups of people sharing common social forms, values, and ways of life. Thus the primary reference is not to political or territorial boundaries, but to boundaries of language, social organization, and beliefs. This is the essential difference between our cross-cultural mode of research and the other common variant of comparative research, the cross-national approach. In cases of sufficient cultural homogeneity we may be dealing with entities such as societies or nation-states, but in many cases we will be referring instead to units such as bands, tribes, and villages that form parts of culturally heterogeneous larger societies.

Anthropologists have written a great deal about the thorny problems associated with cross-cultural sampling (see Naroll, 1970a). How do you measure something vague such as cultural homogeneity well enough to use it as a criterion in sampling? How do you attempt a worldwide cross-cultural sample when the available information on various societies and cultures is so uneven? How do you deal with change over time and the fact that the fullest information about a

13

particular culture may refer to a time after it has substantially changed from its "original" state due to colonial and market contacts? As a sociologist relatively unfamiliar with the available ethnographic sources, I avoided grappling anew with some of these problems by using a preexisting "standard" cross-cultural sample devised by Murdock and White (1969). Reliance on a sample designed by others has the benefit of promoting comparability and cumulation of research findings. Results of previous cross-cultural research have often been hard to compare, given the radically different samples used. (This is a major problem in the compilation of cross-cultural studies presented by Textor, 1967.)

The details on our use of Murdock and White's standard cross-cultural sample are discussed in appendix 1. Here we should mention that this sample is based upon an earlier effort (Murdock, 1968) to map the total universe of known, distinctive cultures. Using criteria of linguistic similarity, cultural resemblance, and geographical contiguity, Murdock grouped over 1,250 known cultures into 200 World Sampling Provinces, designed to represent the known variation in cultures as fully as possible. They used these sampling provinces, with modification, to arrive at the final standard cross-cultural sample of 186 cultures. In most cases one culture was selected from several within each sampling province based upon criteria of quality of ethnographic information, distinctiveness of the culture, or availability of information in the Human Relations Area Files.[1] Thus this sample is an

1. The Human Relations Area Files are a valuable repository of ethnographic studies and information on societies around the world, categorized into several hundred topical areas. The processing of the files takes place at Yale University, and subscribing major university libraries around the country maintain copies of the files. Unfortunately, many known cultures are not contained in the files, and in our sample only 62 of the 93 cultures were included, some of these only partially. For the rest we had to go to the original printed sources, and we did this in most cases even for cultures that were included in HRAF (see appendix 1 for a detailed discussion of our use of sources).

14

effort to systematically cover the known variation in cultures without overlap, while taking into account the problems of data quantity and quality. We have used in our study an alternate case subsample from Murdock and White's original sample, making our sample one with 93 cultures. While the primary reason for using a sample only half as large was our own limited resources, our method makes it possible for others to try to replicate our findings on the other 93 cultures from the standard sample that we didn't use. Since the cultures in Murdock and White's sample are arranged in a sequence of relative cultural similarity (with, for example, cultures 87 and 88 more similar than cultures 87 and 89), an alternate case subsample allows us to reduce problems of interpretation due to the influence of cultural diffusion, known in the technical literature as "Galton's problem" (see Naroll, 1970b). This means that if we discover a relationship between two variables in our sample, it is less likely to have occurred as a result of the accidental joint diffusion of both traits together in our sample than if we had found the same relationship in the full sample. Thus we are trying to minimize the influence of historical contacts between nearby and similar cultures in order to examine patterns of functional relationships and interdependence between different parts of their social organization. We want to know whether low status of women is functionally related to certain cultural traits, rather than having simply diffused together with them from culture to culture by historical accident. Our subsample helps us to do this by minimizing the degree of historical contact between the cultures included even more than does Murdock and White's original sample. Of course no sample can eliminate the effects of diffusion entirely, since this would mean, for example, not including the ancient Romans and the nineteenth-century Comanches in the same sample, since they are linked together by at least one diffused cultural element, the use of the horse. Even by picking only every other culture out of Murdock and White's sample we may not eliminate Galton's problem completely, and we used additional statistical procedures to judge the importance of this problem for our final results (see chapter VI).

The major reason for using cross-cultural samples is that they allow the researcher to examine a much wider range of variation in culture and social structure than studies based on a single society, the comparison of a few societies, or even a large sample of nation-states (the cross-national research mode). Murdock (1957) has shown that, even with a sample of European societies of widely differing times and locations (e.g., the Athenians of 450 B.C., the Icelanders of A.D. 1100, the Boers of the Transvaal in A.D. 1850), the range of cultural and social variation is limited in comparison with a world cross-cultural sample composed of bands, tribes, and states. Even if a study uses nation-states from around the world and not just European ones, the very fact of picking nation-states as a unit for study eliminates most of those preliterate peoples, with their exotic customs, which have long been the focus of anthropological interest. The cross-national mode specifies a certain minimum level of political development and complexity, while the cross-cultural mode does not. If we do not take full advantage of the available variation of world cultures, we cannot be certain that the results and explanations we arrive at will be truly general, rather than applying only to limited types of societies or cultures. A cross-cultural sample allows us to examine cultures from all parts of the world, to look at stateless societies as well as autocratic kingdoms, hunting and gathering as well as farming societies, societies with matrilineal and dual descent as well as those with the patrilineal and bilateral kinship more familiar to us, and so forth. In the case of our subsample of Murdock and White's sample, this means we can consider cultures as diverse as the Kung Bushmen of Africa, the Reindeer Chukchee of Siberia, Babylon at the time of Hammurabi, Cuzco at the height of the Inca empire, and twentieth-century rural villages in Ireland and Japan. (For a complete listing of our sample see appendix 2.)

This wide range of variation also permits cross-cultural

16

researchers to at least flirt with questions of social evolution. The method does not involve following the evolutionary changes in any one culture over millenia, and in fact the time range of information available on most of the cultures included is quite short. However, the cross-cultural method does permit comparisons of cultures that have features that developed comparatively recently on the evolutionary scale (large cities, plow agriculture, written language) with cultures possessing "earlier" traits (roving bands, hunting and gathering subsistence, no written language). There are some problems in making these comparisons, since we don't have a true evolutionary sequence. Simple societies studied today have a history just as long as the peoples in industrial nation-states, and we can't be certain how similar the mode of life of contemporary "primitives" is to that of the hunting and gathering ancestors of today's factory workers and bureaucrats. In dealing with a cross-cultural sample it is therefore not entirely appropriate to talk of early and late or primitive and advanced, as if we had a true evolutionary sequence. Modern researchers avoid this problem by stating hypotheses and generalizations in terms of simple and complex (or relatively undifferentiated and highly differentiated) cultures (see Marsh, 1967; Lenski, 1970), and this is the sort of wording we will employ. We are therefore asking whether certain aspects of the status of women are related to the degree of complexity of the political, economic, and other institutions in a culture, rather than whether there is some clear pattern of change in the status of women over time since before the dawn of recorded history. We also should state that our sample is meant to be representative of all the preindustrial cultures that have been known to exist and about which there is some information, rather than of all the cultures that have ever existed. Many of the latter have disappeared long ago, leaving no historical or even archaeological traces. On the scale of human evolution the cultures included in our sample are all quite recent. The earliest "anthropological present" is 1750 B.C. for Babylon, and for 85

17

out of our 93 cultures the data available refer to a time since A.D. 1800.

The main reason for using a cross-cultural sample is thus the ability to examine large numbers of very diverse cultures. Yet in achieving this we must accept the limitations and problems inherent in the method. One is that the technique severely restricts our handling of variation within particular cultures. We have to make unitary judgments about an entire culture, for instance whether inheritance of property is monopolized by men, shared in varying degrees, or monopolized by women. In a society with substantial variation between classes, urban and rural residents, regions and age groups, it may be difficult, if not impossible, to arrive at such judgments. Women may have equal property rights in the south, and men monopolize such rights in the north, or elite women may have few property rights, while lower-class women have more rights. Special coding instructions are necessary to cope with such problems. Throughout our sample the coding unit is the local settlement or area, rather than the larger society (e.g., Cuzco rather than the entire Inca empire or even the preexpansion Inca state). Within the local settlement, coders were instructed to code generally for the customs of the largest part of the indicated cultural group, which usually means the commoners rather than the elites or despised minorities. (It was not always easy to do this, since in our sample the information on some cultures— particularly Rome and Babylon—referred predominantly to elites.)[2] Even such instructions may not solve all the problems, particularly in communities such as the multicaste villages of India (represented by a village in Uttar Pradesh

2. During the coding of information for this project, two secondary codes were included with each cultural trait coded, one to indicate whether other nearby communities had a different custom from that coded in the community under focus, and another for whether subgroups in the given local community (e.g., elites, minorities) had a different custom. We have not figured out how to make systematic use of these secondary codes, and in this report we rely solely on the primary codes.

in our sample). In such cases no unitary coding may be possible for certain traits, and a coding of "ambiguous" has to be entered. Even when unitary judgments can be arrived at, specialists on a particular culture may feel that using the very broad categories we employ seriously violates the subtlety and complexity of the customs in "their" culture. All of this means that people interested in differences in, and subtle features of, the status of women within societies, say between high and low classes or between rural and urban residents, will find little direct evidence in a cross-cultural study. In such a study the focus is always on cultures as unitary phenomena and the sources of differences among them, not on the sources of variation within each culture.

As a byproduct of this feature of cross-cultural research, the range of evolutionary variation that can be examined is not quite as unlimited as our earlier remarks imply. The necessity of arriving at unitary codings makes it difficult for this type of study to deal with large, complex, industrial societies. We noted in chapter I that our sample consists of preindustrial societies studied mostly by anthropologists with traditional village study techniques. When larger and more complex societies are included, we are dealing either with peasant villages (e.g., the Quiche of Chichicastenango, villages in Ireland, India, and Japan) or the capitals of historic states (e.g., Babylon, Rome, Tenochtitlan of the Aztecs, and Cuzco of the Incas), rather than with the entire society. Murdock and White did make a special effort, however, to include in their sample cultures other than preliterate or tribal ones, and we have already noted that roughly one-third of the sample consists of peasant or urban communities that are part of complex agrarian states (see appendix 4). However, the sample does not include any highly industrialized communities or cities (the closest cases are a Japanese village and a Javanese town, both studied in the 1950s). This limitation means that, insofar as we can generalize about our findings, they will refer to the broad range of preindustrial cultures and communities for the most part, and our range

19

of societal complexity or differentiation will have its highest end "stunted." This also means, of course, that certain aspects of the relative equality or inequality of the sexes that are the focus of interest in studies of complex industrial societies (e.g., relative access to formal education, access to financial credit, wage rates) are not relevant for most of our cultures and do not appear in our data. Thus readers who are primarily interested in why the status of women is different in, say, America, France, and the Soviet Union will find little direct evidence in this study, although indirect inferences and hypotheses may be possible (see chapter VII).

A further byproduct of the "one-code-per-culture" feature is that the resulting statistics have an interpretation that the reader may not be accustomed to, since they refer to the number of cultures in our sample, rather than to the size of the populations or territories involved. A jungle tribe of a few hundred people has an equal weight with cultural units that ruled huge empires (e.g., the Romans and the Incas). Our statistics refer to the percentage of the world's cultures (as reflected in our sample) that follow certain customs, without regard to the number of people, families, or even communities involved. A significant proportion of the world's known cultures depend primarily on hunting and gathering to live, but the percentage of actual people on the earth today who rely on hunting and gathering is much smaller (less than 1%), since these cultures tend to have fewer people than agricultural or industrial societies. This is not so much a limitation of cross-cultural research as simply a feature the reader should keep in mind to avoid misinterpreting our results.

Another feature of a cross-cultural sample, touched on in our discussion of the question of evolution, is that it is cross-sectional. This means that the information about a particular culture refers to one point in time, the designated "anthropological present," and variations over time are largely ignored. In a sense, then, we are comparing snapshots of cultures caught when the anthropologist-photographer happened to pass through. This restriction also results from the need to arrive at unitary codings for traits in particular cultures, since change in traits over time would be difficult to handle.[3] The data available also make this restriction convenient, since for many of the cultures in the sample there is only limited information available for periods before or after the designated anthropological present. Thus the cross-cultural method not only limits our ability to examine the entire sweep of evolutionary change, but also does not permit us to deal easily with changes in particular cultures from year to year and decade to decade. Readers interested in how changes in the status of women come about in particular societies will thus find little direct evidence here, although again perhaps indirect inferences will be possible.

Another problem in the method stems from the nature of the data relied upon, mostly village studies conducted by anthropologists. In some cases the picture we get of a culture in such studies may emphasize the rules and ideals that are supposed to govern people's lives more than the way people actually behave. This is more of a problem in earlier works, when fieldworkers tended to rely more upon individual informants and the products of cultures (e.g., myths and folktales) rather than on prolonged observations of daily life. Since recent training has emphasized techniques of direct observation of behavior, we might suppose that it would be best to include in our sample the most recent studies available on a particular culture. Yet Murdock and White do precisely the opposite, for a very understandable reason. They take in most cases the earliest relatively full descriptions of a particular culture as the anthropological present, the aim being to catch a view of cultures while they were still relatively distinctive, before they were substantially affected by

3. We also included in our coding form two secondary codes for changes over time—one for the case in which a custom had changed during the period prior to the anthropological present, and another for changes since the anthropological present. Again we have yet to devise ways to systematically use this information, and the analysis here relies solely on the primary codes.

21

such forces as colonialism and world-market penetration. (Even with this rule there are many cultures included in the sample that are clearly hybrids of some original elements and later, outside intrusion, such as the horse-using Comanches and the modern-day Quiche of Chichicastenango.) Thus in balancing the desire for more "pristine" cultures and for more modern observational techniques, Murdock and White placed more emphasis on the former. This may lead in some cases to descriptions of cultures that, while relatively full, tend to be idealized.

In some cases this tendency to focus on the ideal and normative elements of a culture may not be a problem, since the rules themselves may be of interest. For instance, we do want to know whether or not a culture has a premarital sexual double standard, regardless of the rates of actual premarital sexual activity of males and females. Yet in some cases in our study this emphasis on the rules and norms does create difficulties. One such problem is that, since most field-workers have been males and their informants more often men than women, we may get a picture of a culture as the men think it is or is supposed to be, which may distort the actual role and status of women (see Goodale, 1971; Wolf, 1972). Another problem is that, by focusing on the formal aspects of the status and rights of women, we may miss the informal power and day-to-day influence that women have in social life. Neither of these problems can be totally solved in a cross-cultural study, but their degree of seriousness can at least be checked. In this study we have coded for a number of "quality control" variables (see Naroll, 1962). One is a code for whether the fieldworkers were exclusively male, exclusively female, or mixed. If we find that women have lower status scores in societies studied exclusively by men, we may conclude that these low scores are due at least partly to the sorts of biases and information loss that occur when information is collected only by males (and perhaps also to the biases and information loss in the other direction to which women fieldworkers are subject in cultures where high scores are registered).[4] We also included codes for the date of the anthropological present, the amount of time spent in the field, the occupation and training of the fieldworkers consulted, and their knowledge of the native language. If we find that the scores for our status of women variable or variables are higher in cultures studied more recently by anthropologists with formal fieldwork training, secure knowledge of the native language, and long periods of time in the field, then we may conclude that part of the reason for low scores obtained in the other cultures is artificial, representing a variation in the way the cultures were studied rather than in the cultures themselves.

The problem of the formal versus informal status of women is not so easily dealt with. In several of our items there were instructions to go beyond the rules and code for actual behavior patterns, e.g., whether women *did* frequently have extramarital affairs. Several other codings asked not for formal holding of offices and such, but for the relative voice (i.e., influence) of males versus females in certain areas of social life (e.g., in arranging marriages). We also included a general item asking whether the authorities used in the study gave any evidence that the informal power and influence of women in a culture was greater than would be apparent from the formal rules and norms of that culture. By looking at both the quality control variables and this latter item we may be able at least to get some idea of how the informal influence of women is related to their formal position. However, this is admittedly a poor substitute for having full information on both the ideals and the daily behavior of men and women for all of the cultures in our sample.

Another feature of the method is the indirect nature of the data one ends up with. Ideally each culture in our sample

4. This reverse bias of female authorities may not be as common as that of males, since most women fieldworkers have not relied as exclusively on female informants as some men have relied on male informants. In some cases, such as Ruth Bunzel in Chichicastenango, women fieldworkers end up using almost exclusively male informants.

should be observed directly, using common instruments and procedures, in order to reduce to a bare minimum the problems of bias introduced by having many different observers with different perspectives and methods. This technique has been attempted by teams studying very limited samples (e.g., in the six-culture study reported in B. Whiting, 1963, and L. Minturn and W. Lambert, 1964), but it is obviously financially impossible with a larger sample. It is temporally impossible as well, since many of the cultures in our sample have either ceased to exist or have been drastically altered by colonialism, industrialism, and other forces for change. In other words, if we wish to use standardized procedures and direct observations we must give up ground on both the size of our sample and its cultural variability. Yet these two traits are the primary assets of cross-cultural research in the first place.

Thus cross-cultural researchers almost universally use second- or third-hand information gathered by anthropologists, explorers, and missionaries, people from different nations and time periods operating with a variety of purposes and methods. Then information about each culture has a long gantlet to run before it ends up as research results. Consider what is involved in our study: First there is the culture out there "as it really is." Then there is the anthropologist, missionary, or explorer who reported on that reality and filtered it through his or her own biases and interests. In some cases the authority did not even observe the culture directly, but asked aged informants "how it is" or even "how it used to be" decades ago. For some of the cultures in our sample (the Kaffa, the Inca, the Aztec, the Callinago) some of the sources used were secondary ones, in which later scholars tried to summarize available primary works, perhaps correcting for some earlier biases but also inserting new ones of their own. In order not to sound too gloomy, it should be noted that there were often several independent primary sources available on a culture at a particular point in time, so that the accuracy of one could be checked against another.

24

(In 66 out of our 93 cultures there was more than one independent source used.)

These often indirect and partial views of cultures were then read and coded by two coders (the detailed coding methods are explained in appendix 1), who had to try to make judgments from what is often scanty information about a wide variety of cultural traits. Again new distortions might be introduced, although there was some check on this through the intercoder agreement scores, which were used as a measure of reliability. Frequent disagreement led to the elimination of some items from subsequent analysis. The final codings arrived at by the two coders led to a single consensus code on each trait (plus a code for intercoder agreement or disagreement), and then these codes were written on coding sheets, punched onto computer cards, and analyzed.

There are many places in this long chain for biases and errors to enter. A particular coding for a culture may represent incorrect field data or careless coding rather than the reality of that culture. The search for maximum cultural variation thus has undeniable costs. The justification for not throwing up one's hands and quitting goes as follows: First, quality of available ethnographic data was one of the basic criteria used by Murdock and White in constructing their sample. Not all of their professional colleagues will agree with their choices, but they have made an effort to rely on the most detailed and accurate sources (within the time constraints discussed earlier). In their article presenting their sample Murdock and White have indicated the names of the preferred authorities for each culture, and for the most part we have followed their preferences. Second, whatever errors and biases occur at various stages are likely to have a randomizing effect; that is, they are likely to decrease the value of all the statistical associations we find, rather than inflate them. In most cross-cultural studies the strength of statistical relationships among variables tends to be fairly low, and our study is no exception. Given the many different kinds of

25

error and bias that can occur, it is unlikely that we will get systematic errors producing spurious relationships. Stated more simply, if predicted relationships are found in spite of the sloppiness of the data and the procedure, then we have reason to feel that we have really found something. We must, of course, still check for the existence of systematic biases. We do this primarily through the records of intercoder agreement and the scores on quality control items. Besides those items already mentioned, we also included codes for the sex of the two coders, the number of sources consulted, the number of separate authorities consulted, the total number of pages in the sources consulted, and the nationality of the authorities. With these codes we can check whether various aspects of the sources we used or the coding process could have contributed in a systematic way to the relationships we observe. (The results of these checks will be reported in chapter VI.)

To summarize, the data we will be using come from all areas of the world and from various time periods. The variation in political and economic forms, marriage customs, and other cultural traits is great, and we can also expect to find in our sample much more variation in the status of women relative to men that we could find in, say, a sample of contemporary nation-states. The size of our sample (93 cultures) allows us to take steps to determine statistically what kinds of political, economic, and other arrangements are found with particular types of high or low status of women. In order to do this we must accept or learn to deal with the limitations and problems of the cross-cultural method as they have been described in the preceding pages.

CHAPTER III

Theories and Predictions

As mentioned in chapter I, at the beginning of our work we scoured the literature for ideas to explain why the status of women might be high in one culture and low in another. We wanted to know whether there are certain cultural or social structural features that are generally associated with such high or low status. (Alternative conceptions would be those of the universalist, who assumes there is little variation from culture to culture, or the rigid historicist, who assumes that the status of women in any culture is the product of the unique historical development of that culture, rather than of any institutional arrangements shared with other cultures.) This led us to a long list of hypotheses we wanted to test.[1]

The final list of hypotheses is given below. The reader will note that they all deal with relations between particular variables and *the* status of women, since they were formulated before we knew what pattern of relationships would emerge among our status variables. If we end up with several scales representing different aspects of the status of women we will have to test our hypotheses separately against each. Our manner of presentation here is to state and explain our hypotheses and then note the cultural traits in our coding form that can be used to test them. These traits are referred to as independent variables since, insofar as we can speak of causa-

---

1. We discuss in this chapter only hypotheses we were able to test. Two ideas we wanted to test but could not were that the relative difference in physical size between men and women and the frequency of childbearing affect the status of women (see Mead, 1949; D'Andrade, 1966, p. 175; Friedl, 1975). Precise data on these topics were available for only 23 and 27 out of our 93 cultures, respectively, so we had to drop these hypotheses from consideration.

tion, we are assuming that these are the societal features that cause the variation from culture to culture in our dependent variables, aspects of the status of women. As mentioned in chapter I, many of the specific variables we use were suggested by, or adapted from, earlier cross-cultural research.

Hypothesis 1a: Women will have lower relative status in cultures where subsistence is based on intensive plow agriculture than in other cultures. (Abbreviated: Intensive Agriculture—)

Hypothesis 1b: Women will have lower status in cultures where subsistence is based on the herding of large animals than in other cultures. (Abbreviated: Animal Herding—)

Hypothesis 1c: Women will have lower status in cultures where subsistence is based on hunting (particularly the hunting of large animals) than in other cultures. (Abbreviated: Hunting—)

This set of hypotheses is based upon the notion that subsistence activities have an importance that ramifies throughout the social system. Tasks that depend a great deal on physical strength, such as hunting, plowing, and the herding of large animals, will be done most often by males (cf. Murdock, 1937), and the monopolization of these tasks will tend to enhance the status of men relative to women. (Another view would be that it is the limitation on the mobility of women caused by childbearing, and not male strength, which makes these male activities.) A variety of cross-cultural and comparative work yields some evidence for one or more of the hypotheses in the set (Hobhouse, Wheeler, and Ginsberg, 1915; Barry, Bacon, and Child, 1957; Textor, 1967, tables 277 and 278; Boserup, 1970). For the case of hunting we are relying mainly on the arguments of Tiger (1969), who, as we saw in chapter I, is more interested in evolutionary universals than in cross-cultural variation. He argues that the requirements of male hunting tend to produce male bonding and solidary men's groups that act to limit the role

28

of women in social life, particularly in political affairs. Tiger feels that, as a result of evolutionary selection processes, men in more complex societies will continue to exhibit such bonding and exclusionary tendencies, tendencies imprinted on men genetically by their early years as hunters. However, if these arguments are correct we can surmise that such tendencies should be more true of societies still relying heavily on hunting than of those who depended on hunting only at some time in their dim, evolutionary pasts. Thus we are led to a cross-cultural hypothesis that the status of women will be lower where hunting is important for subsistence than where it is not.

A number of variables included in our coding form can help us to test these relationships:[2]

Indicators for hypothesis 1a: Intensive Agriculture—

Independent variable (hereafter IV) 1:
   The plow (absence or presence)

IV 2:   Irrigation (absence or presence)

IV 3:   Cereal grains the principal crop (no or yes)

IV 4:   Roots and tubers the principal crops (no or yes)

IV 5:   Tree fruits and starches the principal crops (no or yes)

IV 6:   Relative importance of agriculture in subsistence (a 5-point scale ranging from insignificant to dominant)

The first three independent variables measure items usually associated with intensive plow agriculture, although there are exceptions (e.g., corn cultivation often takes place using simply a digging stick or hoe). Tree and root crop independent variables are intended to locate cultures with agri-

2. The actual wording of the form used to code for our variables and the accompanying instructions are not reproduced here, but are available to interested scholars upon request.

culture that is extensive rather than intensive, and according to the hypothesis we expect these primary crops (which are not usually felt to take as much strength) to be associated with *higher* status for women. The general agricultural code (IV 6) does not make this distinction, but is designed to measure the relative importance of any sort of agricultural activity. Taken together, these six variables should allow us to examine the relationship between both agriculture in general and specific types of agriculture and the status of women.

Indicators for hypothesis 1b: Animal Herding—

IV 7:   Large nonmilked aboriginal domestic animals (absence or presence)

IV 8:   Large milked aboriginal domestic animals (absence or presence)

IV 9:   Small aboriginal domestic animals—excluding dogs, cats, fowl, guinea pigs (absence or presence)

IV 10:   Large domestic animals, only since European contact (absence or presence)

IV 11:   Small domestic animals only since European contact (absence or presence)

IV 12:   Importance of animal husbandry in subsistence (a 5-point scale ranging from insignificant to dominant)

Here again we can look at both animal husbandry in general as well as the effects of different types of animal raising on the status of women.

Indicators for hypothesis 1c: Hunting—

IV 13:   Large animals are hunted and important to the diet (no or yes)

IV 14:   Small animals are hunted and important to the diet (no or yes)

IV 15: Intermediate animals are hunted and important to the diet (no or yes)

IV 16: Importance of hunting and gathering in subsistence (a 5-point scale ranging from insignificant to dominant)

Again we can use these separate items to look not only at hunting in general, but at the effects of hunting animals of different sizes.

Hypothesis 2a: Women will have lower status in cultures with constant warfare than in other cultures. (Abbreviated: Warfare—)

Hypothesis 2b: Women will have higher status in cultures with constant warfare than in other cultures. (Abbreviated: Warfare+)

Hypothesis 2a is based upon reasoning similar to the first set of hypotheses. Warfare requires strength, aggressiveness, and speed, traits that are generally associated with males. Women also are not able to be warriors due to the burdens of pregnancy and nursing. Where warfare is more common the role of men should be more highly valued along with male qualities, and the status of men should be higher (see Murdock, 1949, p. 205). A more psychological version of this argument is that where warfare is very frequent, women and men will of necessity rear their sons to be violent and aggressive, and when they grow up males will display these traits not only against external enemies, but against their own spouses. Thus warfare will require women to raise male children who will dominate their wives absolutely (see Harris, 1974, pp. 83ff.). Other reasoning leads us to the opposite prediction in hypothesis 2b. Where warfare is very common men may be so involved in fighting that they will have little time for producing food or supervising the sex lives of their wives and daughters. In such societies women should have more status and influence. In other words hypothesis 2b

31

suggests a "Rosie-the-riveter" effect as a cross-cultural regularity. Here we have only one item to serve as our independent variable:

Indicators for hypotheses 2a and 2b: Warfare— and +

IV 17:   Frequency of intercommunity armed conflict— a 2-point scale—past, supralocal, or absent local warfare versus present or endemic local warfare (collapsed from an original five categories)

Hypothesis 3: In cultures with a high degree of institutionalized male solidarity, women will have lower status than in other cultures. (Abbreviated: Male Solidarity—)

Here we are relying on the arguments of Tiger (1969) and the empirical work of Young (1965). They suggest that a particular mechanism by which men dominate women is the forming of intense collective solidarities among men from which women are excluded, examples being men's secret societies, clubs, and male initiation ceremonies. In societies where such forms of male solidarity are strongly developed, they may have the effect of excluding women from certain areas of social life, perhaps indicating the ritual and collective inferiority of women. For independent variables here we have two Guttman scales[3] composed of items indicating the strength of the traits involved:

3. Guttman scales are ordinal (i.e., ordered) scales constructed from a number of traits, all of which are coded present or absent. The assumption is that these items form a natural hierarchy such that, if a higher item is found present, all of the lower items will also be found present. In the male initiation ceremony scale, if beating or hazing of initiates is found, then we expect to also find personal dramatization of the initiates and organized social response, and if we did not this would be scored as one or more errors in the scale. Only if this sort of pattern emerges regularly, with few errors, will the scale meet the acceptable scaling criterion (a minimum coefficient of scalability of .65) to be used. See Young, 1965, chapter 3, for a discussion of Guttman scaling in cross-cultural research.

Indicators for hypothesis 3: Male Solidarity—

IV 18:   Initiation ceremonies for adolescent males—a 5-item scale ranging from no initiation to minimal social recognition, personal dramatization of the initiate, organized social response, and finally, affective social response—i.e., beating or hazing or operations (coefficient of scalability = .76)

IV 19:   Male solidarity[4]—a 5-item scale ranging from no institutionalized male solidarity to some exclusive male activity protected by physical or normative barriers, ritualization given to this activity, definite ranking of men within this activity, and finally, war training or planning a part of this activity (coefficient of scalability = .88)

Hypothesis 4a: In cultures with matrilineal descent, women will have higher status than in other cultures. (Abbreviated: Matrilineal Descent+)

Hypothesis 4b: In cultures with matrilocal postmarital residence rules, women will have higher status than in other cultures. (Abbreviated: Matrilocal Residence+)

4. It should be mentioned here that Young and Bacdayan (1965) considered male solidarity as part of a larger concept they refer to as social rigidity, which they define (p. 230) as "the relative lack of intercommunication among the parts of the [social] system"—in other words institutional arrangements that tend to separate parts of the community, in this case men from women. They proceeded to form an additional Guttman scale of social rigidity, in which the presence of minimal male solidarity was followed by items for the subcommunity having a sacred focus, for subcommunity exogamy, and for the existence of banishment from the group as a punishment for violations of communal norms. We wanted to include a scale of social rigidity in our study as well, but the items indicated did not meet the minimum condition of scalability—a coefficient of scalability of at least .65. Perhaps this is because our data were collected at the community or settlement level, while Young and Bacdayan coded information at the subcommunity level.

33

As mentioned briefly in chapter I, there is a continuing debate within the anthropological literature about the significance of rules of descent and postmarital residence for the status of women. Many nineteenth-century evolutionary anthropologists took the customs of tracing kin-group membership through women or living with the wife's family after marriage as evidence of an earlier evolutionary stage in which women had reigned supreme (see Bachofen, 1861; Engels, 1902). When evolutionary theorizing came under attack around the turn of the century this position was repudiated and replaced by the view cited in chapter I that descent rules or postmarital residence preferences make little difference in the general status of women. In matrilineal and matrilocal societies, as in others, the status of women may vary in many ways, while men still monopolize positions of authority (see Lowie, 1920, chapter VIII). However, more recently a number of anthropologists have come to the conclusion that matrilineal descent and matrilocal residence are both associated with at least somewhat better status for women, although not the sort of exalted status once theorized by nineteenth-century evolutionists (cf. Murdock, 1949, p. 205; Gough, 1972; Schlegel, 1972). There is also a debate in the literature about whether descent, which involves kin-group membership, or postmarital residence, which determines who actually lives together, is more significant for other features of the social structure. We include both here.

Indicators for hypothesis 4a: Matrilineal Descent+

IV 20:   Descent—collapsed into a 2-category scale— patrilineal, dual, bilateral, or other descent versus matrilineal

Indicators for hypothesis 4b: Matrilocal Residence+

IV 21:   Residence—collapsed into a 2-category scale— all other residence rules versus matrilocal[5]

5. It is assumed that the crucial factor with residence rules is whether or not women continue to live with their female kin after

34

Hypothesis 5: Women will have lower status in cultures that favor large extended families than in cultures that favor nuclear families. (Abbreviated: Extended Families—)

A number of arguments in the literature point to the importance of the size and structure of the family in determining the position of women (see Engels, 1902; Boserup, 1970; Barry, Bacon, and Child, 1957; Zelman, 1974). The larger the family, so one argument goes, the more it will require or develop a hierarchical rather than an egalitarian set of internal relationships; and since where hierarchies develop men tend to dominate them, such large families will place women in a more subordinate status than will smaller families. Another argument stresses not authority, but competence. In a large family there will be several adults of both sexes. When this is the case it is more likely for a sharp sexual division of labor to develop, since if some members of one sex are absent others of the same sex can substitute for them. In a nuclear family, in contrast, there will only be the husband and his wife or wives, and each adult will have to be more of a "jack-of-all-trades" and be willing to substitute for the other, since no other adults will be easily available. The husband will therefore depend heavily upon his wife (or wives), and she will develop the ability to do many things that are ordinarily done by males. As a result, the woman is less likely to be dominated and oppressed. This argument can be generalized from the individual family level to the entire society, since some cultures favor maintaining large extended families, while others, such as our own, prefer the nuclear family arrangement. We will test this hypothesis with a variable adopted from Murdock's work, one that classifies the

---

marriage. Therefore a type of residence favored in some matrilineal societies, avunculocal residence, in which a male moves in with his maternal uncle and brings his bride to live there also, is assumed to have no special positive effect on the status of women and is grouped with other rules, rather than with matrilocal residence.

35

family form that is favored in a given society. (A variable for the actual average number of people—or adults—per family would in some ways be preferable, since we know that a large proportion of families are nuclear even in societies that favor extended families. Unfortunately the required statistics are not available for most of the cultures in our sample.)

Indicators for hypothesis 5: Extended Families—

IV 22: Preferred family form—a 4-point variable, ranging from nuclear through stem and lineal to extended (adapted from Murdock, 1961)

Hypothesis 6: Women will have lower status in cultures with complex political hierarchies such as the state or an autocratic kingdom than in other cultures. (Abbreviated: Political Hierarchy—)

A number of writers point out the importance of the type of political structure for the rights and status of women (Murdock, 1949, p. 205; Stephens, 1963, chapter 7; Gough, 1972). The arguments vary somewhat, but generally relate to the fact that, since men tend to dominate whatever political hierarchies emerge, the more developed the hierarchy, the more men will be able to use it to dominate women, and the greater the tendency for autocratic relations between ruler and subject to be reflected in similar relations between man and wife. There is some ambiguity in the available literature, since Collins (1971) says that women will fare better in a state (with governmental monopoly on the legitimate use of force as the defining criterion) than in what he calls a fortified society, which seems to be a feudal society in which men can more freely use physical force against their wives and daughters. Also Millett (1969, p. 158), citing Bertrand Russell, states that under some conditions a strong state is associated with a weak family and better status for women. Nevertheless, it seems best here to leave our hypothesis in the form suggested by the bulk of the literature.

Indicators for hypothesis 6: Political Hierarchy—

IV 23: Political organization—a 5-point scale ranging from absence of local political integration to a state form (defined here as political integration in a unit of 100,000 or more people—adapted from Murdock, 1961, p. 207)

IV 24: Crimes versus person punished—a 2-point scale —by person or group wronged versus by government action.

IV 25: Government—a 2-point scale—full-time bureaucrats unrelated to government head absent or present[6]

IV 26: Community part of a kingdom—no or yes (defined as a centralized political unit with centralized organs of political control, power to tax, and rule concentrated in a single office, which is hereditary—following Stephens, 1963)

IV 27: Community part of a kingdom in the past that no longer exists (no or yes)

Hypothesis 7: Women will have lower status in cultures possessing significant private property rights in the means of production than in cultures lacking the same. (Abbreviated: Private Property—)

This hypothesis stems from the arguments presented by Engels (1902) to the effect that when private property emerges, men tend to monopolize it and use that possession to reduce wives and daughters to submission and dependence, much as the later capitalist did to the proletariat (see also Gough, 1972; Murdock, 1949, p. 205). It should be noted

6. Variables IV 24 and IV 25 form part of a Guttman scale of societal complexity devised by Freeman and Winch, 1957, which will be mentioned shortly. They are included here as separate items because of their specific relationship to political complexity.

that various writers disagree on what types of property are important, particularly land or movable property, such as animals or slaves. Here we have included just one general item.

Indicator for hypothesis 7: Private Property—

IV 28:   Private property in the means of production (absence or presence)

It should be noted that neither hypothesis 6 nor 7 by itself can explain why it is the men who benefit. One can imagine autocratic queendoms leading to local female dominance, and women as holders of private property dominating their "proletarian" husbands and sons. Clearly these hypotheses, even if confirmed, would not explain why it is the men who are dominant in the first place. They only say that such domination will be greater where political hierarchies and private property are important.

Hypothesis 8: In more complex and differentiated cultures women will have lower status than in less complex cultures. (Abbreviated: Complexity—)

The reasoning here is somewhat vaguer than with our previous hypotheses. It starts by noting that several of the variables already mentioned (plow agriculture, the state, private property rights) are indicators of at least intermediate ranges in societal complexity or differentiation, as these concepts have been used in discussing social evolution (see Marsh, 1967; Lenski, 1970).[7] Furthermore, a number of recent studies of some family variables suggest that there are

7. The concepts of complexity and differentiation refer to the general recognition of the fact that there is much more specialization in roles and organizations, and much more varied and efficient technology, in modern industrial societies than in preindustrial societies. In the simplest hunting and gathering societies one can observe today, there are no political organizations apart from kinship collectivities (such as lineages and clans), while more complex societies have non-kin-based political institutions, themselves divided into spe-

systematic relationships between these variables and aspects of societal complexity and differentiation (e.g., for premarital sexual restrictions see Murdock, 1970; for family structure see Nimkoff and Middleton, 1960, and Blumberg and Winch, 1972; for monogamy versus polygyny see Osmond, 1964). The patterns discerned vary, the most common being some sort of direct linear relationship (e.g., with more complexity, more restrictions on premarital sex) or some sort of curvilinear relationship (e.g., with complex industrial societies more like the simplest societies in favoring nuclear families over extended families, and less like the intermediate societies). Finally, much of the general literature on the status of women is primarily concerned with the effects of "the march of civilization" and social evolution on the status of women (see Bachofen, 1861; Hobhouse, 1924, volume 1, chapter 4; Engels, 1902; Gough, 1972; Morgan, 1972). These bits of evidence and speculation suggest that it would be worthwhile to examine the relationship between some general indicators of societal complexity and the status of women. We should reiterate a point from chapter II, that with our sample we are not able to examine evolution over long periods in particular cultures, or even to examine the impact of recent "modernization." What we can do is examine whether cultures with certain kinds of institutional and cultural differentiation have lower women's status scores than simpler cultures. Since, as mentioned in chapter II, our sample is heavily concentrated in the simple and intermediate ranges in complexity (lacking highly industrialized communities), we feel we can ignore the curvilineal trends represented by possible improvements in the status of women in the most complex societies and hypothesize a direct linear, and negative, relationship. We can assemble a long list of societal complexity variables to examine

---

cialized agencies and hierarchical levels. When we refer to simple and complex here it is in this technical sense, and its use does not imply that people in simpler societies are simpleminded, or that these simple societies do not have other kinds of complexities of their own—for example in marriage regulations and kinship terminologies.

this hypothesis, including some that we have already dealt with:

Indicators for hypothesis 8: Complexity—

IV 1:   Plow (absence or presence)

IV 2:   Irrigation (absence or presence)

IV 3:   Cereal grains the principal crops (no or yes)

IV 6:   Importance of agriculture in subsistence (a 5-point scale)

IV 23:   Political organizations (a 5-point scale)

IV 28:   Private property (absence or presence)

IV 29:   Settlement type (a 5-point scale ranging from migratory bands to complex settlements surrounded by homesteads or hamlets considered part of the community)

IV 30:   Metalworking (absence or presence)

IV 31:   Manufacturing of pottery (absence or presence)

IV 32:   True weaving (absence or presence)

IV 33:   Social stratification in the larger society (a 4-point scale ranging from lack of significant stratification to complex stratification into three or more classes)

IV 34:   Social stratification in the local settlement—the same categories as in IV 33

IV 35:   Societal complexity (a 6-point Guttman scale adapted from Freeman and Winch, 1957, ranging from the absence of all traits through crimes punished by government action, full-time specialized priests present, formal education present, written language present, and finally, full-time bureaucrats unrelated to the government head—coefficient of scalability for this scale is .643, a shade below the usually accepted minimum of .65)

We should note that these variables refer to traits that fit at rather diverse points in conceptions of human evolution— e.g., metalworking and pottery making came much earlier than the plow. This variety permits us to examine not only whether increasing complexity is related in general to lower status for women, but whether some watersheds are more important than others.

Hypothesis 9: Women will have lower status in cultures where classical religions are practiced (Christianity, Islam, Hinduism, Buddhism) than in cultures with preclassical religions. (Abbreviated: Classical Religion—)

One recurring line of theorizing suggests that religious ideology has a crucial influence over the status of women. Some nineteenth-century writers felt that Christianity, with its doctrines of monogamy, marriage stability, and sexual restrictions, played an important role in upgrading the position of women in cultures where it was introduced by missionaries and colonialists. More recently, however, feminist writers have pointed to the strong masculine bias in the religious doctrines of most if not all of the world's major religions (see Ruether, 1974). Such writers see these doctrines as having a negative effect on women in both complex societies and in the simpler societies where they have been newly introduced. The available sociological research (e.g., Goode, 1963) makes this point most strongly about Islam, but there are suggestions that other major religions also have an influence that favors men. In line with these latter arguments, we wish to investigate whether cultures where such major religions are practiced do, in fact, accord women lower status. In reference to our previous hypothesis dealing with complexity, we also want to know whether any relationship that may exist between complexity and the status of women is due to the influence of such religious doctrines (since they are most often found in the complex cultures in our sample) or to other factors. We use a single 3-point variable to test this hypothesis.

41

Indicator for hypothesis 9: Classical Religion—

IV 36: Religion practiced—3 points, ranging from cultures with preclassical religions through cultures with a mixture of classical and preclassical to those with classical religions

Hypothesis 10a: Low status of women is associated with a high degree of institutionalized envy between the sexes. (Abbreviated: Envy—)

Hypothesis 10b: High status of women is associated with a high degree of institutionalized envy between the sexes. (Abbreviated Envy+)

The argument for hypothesis 10a is that men fear the power of women, for example their control over children and sexual favors, and, in their desire to free themselves from that power, they will strive to control women's lives. The higher the amount of envy and fear men have of women, the greater will be their efforts to control women (see Murphy, 1959; Montagu, 1968; Bettelheim, 1954). The reasoning for hypothesis 10b looks at the same phenomenon the other way around. Where women have more power, men will envy and fear them more. Thus the greater the power and influence of women, the more we are likely to find institutionalized expressions of male envy and anxiety (see Levine, 1966). The problem in testing these ideas rests in how to find indicators of institutionalized envy between the sexes. The literature of psychoanalytically oriented anthropologists abounds with customs thought to reflect—or produce—fear and envy between the sexes. In our coding form we included the following items: genital operations performed on males at initiation, genital operations performed on females at initiation (Bettelheim, 1954); exaggerated couvade customs in which males simulate labor pains and recovery; exclusive mother-infant and exclusive mother-child sleeping arrangements (Anthony, 1955; Whiting, Kluckhohn, and Anthony, 1958); ceremonies in which men imitate women; ceremonies in which women imitate men; and a Guttman scale of menstrual taboo customs (from Stephens, 1962—see chapter IV for fuller details). It turned out that most of these items were not strongly associated with each other, casting doubt on whether these customs do have a connection with institutionalized envy between the sexes. Four items were, however, sufficiently related for combination into a single scale: men imitate women, women imitate men, exclusive mother-infant sleeping, and exclusive mother-child sleeping (all coded absent or present). These were combined with equal weights to produce a 3-point scale for institutionalized envy:

Indicators for hypotheses 10a and 10b: Envy— and +

IV 37:   Institutionalized envy (a 3-point scale—average inter-item correlation of the four items = .29)

Hypothesis 11a: Women will have higher status in cultures where there is a shortage of women than in other cultures. (Abbreviated: Female Shortage+)

Hypothesis 11b: Women will have higher status in cultures where men are absent for long periods of time than in other cultures. (Abbreviated: Male Absence+)

Both hypotheses here deal with the effects on status of the sheer numbers of women versus men, or their availability in the local settlement. Hypothesis 11a follows the logic that if women are scarce, men will have to compete for them and treat them more kindly, and women will be able to take advantage of this situation to improve their status. Hypothesis 11b is just a general restatement of the idea underlying hypothesis 2b, that when men are absent from the community for long periods, for warfare or other reasons, this will tend to increase the importance and power of the women (see Mencher, 1965, on the Nayar; Wallace, 1971, on the Iroquois). Unfortunately most of the sources we are using have

43

nothing close to detailed population statistics, so for the most part we rely in testing hypothesis 11a on general statements about excesses of males or females.

Indicator for hypothesis 11a: Female Shortage+

IV 38: Sex ratio (a 3-point scale from female excess to male excess)

Indicator for hypothesis 11b: Male Absence+

IV 39: Systematic absences of males—a 3-point scale ranging from no systematic absences to systematic absences common presently

Up to now we have treated the world as if there were a set of neatly defined independent variables that could affect the relative status of women and another set of neatly defined variables that represent aspects of the status of women itself (i.e., our dependent variables). Unfortunately the world, or at least the world of previous theorists, is not so neat. Whether a variable is viewed as independent or dependent is in many cases simply a question of theoretical preference. Also, many writers describe some particular aspect of the status of women as crucial to their standing in all other areas. If, according to this view, women gain certain crucial rights or powers relative to men, then they will have high status in society generally, regardless of whether the society is matrilineal or patrilineal, agrarian or hunting, and so forth. The most commonly stated crucial variables are women's share in the inheritance and control of property (Engels, 1902; Sacks, 1971), women's collective work organization (ibid.), women's contribution to subsistence (Boserup, 1970), the control by women of the fruits of the labor of men and women (Engels, 1902; Brown, 1970; Friedl, 1975), and the presence or absence of polygyny (Textor, 1970, table 277). The details of the arguments in the literature will not be restated here except to note that we derive two contrary hypotheses for women's contribution to subsistence, since it has

44

been argued both that if women produce much of a culture's food they will gain in status, and, on the contrary, that if they produce much of a culture's food they are being exploited by lazy men.[8] Also while our hypothesis states, and most nineteenth-century evolutionists thought, that polygyny is related to the degradation of women, more recently scholars have questioned whether it has such negative effects at all (cf. Clignet, 1970).

Hypothesis 12: The greater the control women have over the valuable property in a culture, the higher will be their general status. (Abbreviated: Women's Property+)

IV 40: Inheritance rights[9]—a 4-point scale from predominant male inheritance to predominant female inheritance

Hypothesis 13: In cultures where woman are organized collectively for economic activities their general status will be higher than in other cultures. (Abbreviated: Women's Work Organization+)

IV 41: Villagewide, exclusively female work groups—absence or presence

Hypothesis 14a: In cultures where women contribute much to subsistence, their general status will be higher than where women contribute little (Abbreviated: Subsistence Role+)

8. It is interesting to note that the logic behind hypothesis 14a is the same as that underlying hypotheses 1a-1c, dealing with male subsistence activities. However, to my knowledge nobody has presented hypotheses converse to 1a-1c, following the logic of hypothesis 14b, i.e., where men contribute much to subsistence the status of women will be high. In other words the existing literature generally takes the position that women are damned if they do (do most of the work) and damned if they don't. We can at least examine whether this is true.

9. As will be explained in more detail in chapter IV, we originally included four property control variables in this study, but only this item for inheritance rights showed sufficient intercoder agreement to be used.

45

Hypothesis 14b: In cultures where women contribute much to subsistence their general status will be lower than where they contribute little. (Abbreviated: Subsistence Role—)

IV 42: The relative contribution of women to subsistence —a 7-point scale (for details on its construction see chapter IV)

Hypothesis 15: In cultures where women have substantial control over the fruits of productive labor their general status will be higher than where they have little control. (Abbreviated: Control Fruits+)

IV 43: Control over the fruits of male labor—a 4-point scale ranging from sole male control to predominant female control

IV 44: Control over the fruits of joint labor—a 4-point scale

IV 45: Control over the fruits of female labor—a 4-point scale

Hypothesis 16: In cultures with polyandry or monogamy women will have higher status in general than in cultures with polygyny. (Abbreviated: Polyandry+)

IV 46: Preferential marriage form—a 4-point scale ranging from general polygyny (polygynous unions in excess of 20% of all unions) through limited polygyny and monogamy to polyandry

We will see independent variables 40-46 again in the guise of dependent variables in chapters IV and V. Once again there is nothing wrong with considering these variables in both ways, since to a large extent these labels are a matter of theoretical preference. Essentially we are setting off variables IV 40-IV 46 as a special group that may have some crucial mediating role between our other independent variables and the general status of women.

No doubt other hypotheses could be derived, but the 16

already listed exhaust the most frequently cited forces affecting the status of women, and probably exhaust (or surpass) our ability to analyze our empirical results as well. Clearly we have established a broad range of competing explanations with which to attack the question of why the status of women varies from one culture to another. However, we must still deal with the possibility that the variations in our measures of the status of women are due not to the kinds of social structural factors dealt with in these hypotheses, but to problems in our sources and data collection procedures (see the discussion in chapter II), or to factors of regional variation and historical diffusion that have nothing to do with social structure. We test these possibilities by forming new hypotheses for relationships between our quality control variables (termed CV below) and our measure or measures of the status of women.

Hypothesis 17: Variation in the relative status of women in our sample is an artifact produced by problems in our sources and in our data collection techniques. (Abbreviated: Data Quality+)

CV 1:   Sex of coders—a 3-point scale from both male to both female

CV 2:   Number of sources consulted—a 5-point scale from 1 to 6-9

CV 3:   Number of authorities consulted—a 4-point scale from 1 to 4-7

CV 4:   Total pages in the sources consulted—a 4-point scale from under 300 to over 1,000

CV 5:   Sex of authorities—a 2-point scale—all males versus mixed male and female or all female

CV 6:   Nationality of authorities—a 3-point scale from all Americans to all non-Americans

CV 7:   Occupation of authorities—a 3-point scale from no anthropologists to all anthropologists

47

CV 8: Formal fieldwork training of authorities—a 3-point scale from none had to all had

CV 9: Knowledge of the native language—a 3-point scale from none of the authorities knew it well to all knew it well

CV 10: Total periods of fieldwork—a 3-point scale from one year or less to more than three years

CV 11: Anthropological present—a 4-point scale from before A.D. 1800 to after A.D. 1950

Hypothesis 18: Variation in the relative status of women in our sample is an artifact produced by simple regional variation and the patterns of historical diffusion of cultural traits.

CV 12: Region—six categories from Sub-Saharan Africa to South America

That regional variations exist in some of the variables we are interested in is clear (see Boserup, 1970, on regional differences in male versus female farming and market activity). What is not clear is whether these are general regional patterns unrelated to the social structural differences among cultures within a region. If an association between regions and our measures of the status of women turns up, we will need to examine the combined effect of region and some of our independent variables on the status of women. Using the regional variable CV 12 will not detect all the diffusion effects that we need to control for and in chapter VI we will discuss the results of statistical checks on the importance of these effects—tests for the seriousness of what is referred to as "Galton's problem."

The set of independent variables presented in this chapter in combination with these control variables give us the ability to examine in detail many competing ideas about why women have higher status relative to men in some societies than in others.

CHAPTER IV

How the Status of Women Varies

WE have now specified some features of the way societies are organized that we think may affect the status of women, and in this chapter we will examine the kinds of variations that we will be trying to explain. In other words, before we can test why the status of women varies cross-culturally, we must clarify how it varies, and we will do this by examining one by one the 52 dependent variable items we think may have some relationship to our general concept of the status of women. In these pages we will follow a rough order through items dealing with religion, politics, economics, family and sexual matters, and other topics, where possible relating the cross-cultural patterns we find to those discovered in earlier research. It should be noted that the wording in some of the categories for our 52 items may seem confusing because two or more categories from our original coding form have been collapsed together for purposes of analysis, due to the small number of cultures coded in each category. This may also give some of the items listed here the appearance of prior bias in favor of men or women, whereas in fact the original coding form used exactly symmetrical categories (for example, categories of "exclusively male" and "exclusively female" were included even if we expected to find many instances of the former and no instances of the latter).

Our purpose in presenting the frequency distributions of these dependent variable items here is to give some idea of how different aspects of the relative status of women are distributed cross-culturally. We will in the process mention some items that will not be of interest to us in subsequent stages of this work. Some items will not be used beyond this chapter because of reliability or lack of information problems, and some will not enter the scale or scales of the status of women we will construct in chapter V, but the distribution of these items in our sample is still of interest. We should also mention once again that we have purposefully conceived of the status of women broadly, and some items discussed below may have only the vaguest logical link with popular conceptions of the relative power, influence, rights, and importance of women. Rather than prejudge the issue by defining the status of women narrowly and using a few items selected to fit that definition, we prefer to leave the matter open and use empirical methods (in chapter V) to see how these many items relate to each other. (Throughout the chapter percentages are rounded off for ease in reading.)

RELIGION

DV 1: Sex of gods and spirits and other supernatural beings[1]

	No. of cultures	%
1. All male	9	13
2. Both, but male are more numerous or more powerful or both	24	36
3. Both, with male more numerous while power equal, or male more powerful while numbers equal	13	19
4. Both, and equal in numbers or power or both, or women more numerous but power equal, or women more powerful but numbers equal	21	31
5. Sex of gods and spirits unascertainable	26	—
Total	93	99

In spite of the emphasis in the writings of theorists of matriarchy on the prevalence of female gods in early socie-

1. As in the previous chapter abbreviated wording is used to describe each variable here. The full wording used in the original coding form can be obtained on request from the author.

ties (Davis, 1971), we see in our sample a range from solely male gods and spirits to rough equality, and we found no cultures with solely female gods and spirits. Category 4 here is collapsed from 20 cases of equality of male and female spirits and only one case (the Marquesans) of slight female predominance. Thus our finding accords roughly with the observation of Goldberg (1973, p. 177) that in fact cultures with predominant female gods are a rarity. Yet we note, as Goldberg does not, since he is focusing on the universality of male dominance, that equality in numbers and powers of male and female spirits is quite a common pattern. An item on mythical founders reveals a similar pattern:

DV 2: Mythical founders of the culture

	No. of cultures	%
1. All were male	22	34
2. Both sexes, but the role of men more important	17	26
3. Both sexes, and the role of both sexes pretty equal	20	31
4. Both sexes, but female role more important, or solely female	6	9
5. No such myth, or no information	28	—
Total	93	100

Again category 4 is collapsed from five cultures for which female mythical founders were judged more important and only one culture (Truk) coded as having solely female mythical founders. We see here a pattern that will frequently recur in this chapter: items ranging from male predominance to rough equality of the sexes, with few if any cultures coded for female predominance.

We also included codes for the relative sexes of priests (defined as religious specialists officiating at rituals for the entire community), shamans (individuals performing religious and magical services for the benefit of individual clients) and witches (individuals performing religious and magical acts to harm individuals). The item for priests was more heavily biased toward male predominance than our previous items (38 cultures were coded as having exclusively male priests), but since priests were lacking or information was lacking for 35 out of our 93 cultures, we rejected the use of this item in our dependent variable pool. (We chose as our arbitrary criterion of exclusion items for which there were codings on less than two-thirds of our sample, or 62 cultures.) This leaves the items for shamans and witches.

DV 3:   Sex of shamans

	No. of cultures	%
1. All are male	14	19
2. Both, but male more numerous, more powerful, or both	26	36
3. Both, but male more numerous, while female equally powerful, or male more powerful while female equally numerous, or about equal in numbers or power or both	26	36
4. Both, but female more powerful or more numerous or both, or solely female shamans	7	10
5. No shamans, or no information	20	—
Total	93	101

DV 4:   Sex of reputed witches

	No. of cultures	%
1. All male	16	24
2. Both, but male predominance in numbers or power or both	21	31
3. Both, and equal in numbers or power or both	23	34

4. Both, but female predominance in numbers or power or both, or only female witches	8	12
5. No information or no belief in witches	25	—
Total	93	101

We note similar distributions for these two items, which are both skewed toward male predominance, although neither has as many cultures coded as "solely male" as our rejected item of priests (38 cultures). This difference corresponds with the generalization often made that the more a cultural trait concerns broader groupings and access to leadership in larger collectivities, the more it will tend to be dominated by males. (The criterion of community versus individual religious services was the distinction made between our item for priests and our item for shamans.)

At the same time the distribution we find on DV 4 is perhaps less expected. We often find statements in the literature that witchcraft is most often attributed to females (as it has been in our culture) and reflects the kind of envy and fear of the power of women referred to in hypothesis 10 in the preceding chapter. Margaret Mead states (1971, p. 54):

> It is true that witchcraft is not confined to women. . . . Nevertheless, witchcraft is most closely associated with things that are feared about a woman: the elusive quality of beauty and charm; the belief that the woman who yields in a man's arms has only lent herself to him for her own dangerous purposes or that the woman sleeping by a man's side is really somewhere else in mind and spirit, leaving behind only an empty shell; the fear that the midwife may snatch away the newborn or cause it to die or that a woman's hand, stretched out in apparent compassion, may do deadly injury.

We find, unlike Mead, that the general pattern cross-culturally is for witches to be equally of both sexes, or to be somewhat more commonly men than women. Some of this difference may be due to the fact that Mead defined witchcraft somewhat differently than we did. She states in the same article that witches are born that way and do evil in spite of themselves. As such they can be distinguished from sorcerers, who have learned to perform evil magic. In our coding we did not distinguish between witches and sorcerers in this sense, and it is not clear that this is a distinction that is generally made in the cultures in our sample. Our coding lumps together in one category people with both innate and acquired abilities to perform evil magic. Even so, it is interesting to note that our results do not give us reason to expect that the performance of evil black magic represents a manifestation of fear of the power of women.

We see that the most common pattern is for men to be viewed as more likely to engage in witchcraft than women. We have noted the similarity of the cross-cultural distributions of the items for shamans and witches. We stress again that our coding instructions defined the difference between these two roles as whether they involved the ability to manipulate supernatural forces to benefit or to harm individuals. Of course in practice in many societies these two roles are combined; practitioners can use their mystical powers to aid certain individuals while at the same time they employ them (or are suspected of doing so) to harm others. Whether the roles are seen as combined or not, the targets of evil magic are not consistently of one sex or the other. In societies where belief in witchcraft is pronounced, both men and women live in fear of falling victim. What witchcraft usually suggests, then, is not a manifestation of sexual anxiety or envy, but simply the existence of certain special mystical gifts or powers, often used for good and evil, which distinguish those who possess them. By that possession they gain a certain amount of awe and respect from their fellow tribesmen or villagers. When special powers are involved, whether they are mystical as here or of a political or other nature, as we shall see later, men are more likely to possess them than women. However, we see from both items that exclusive possession of such powers by men is not that common a pattern.

54

An item for participation in religious ceremonies shows once again a pattern of male predominance more common than female predominance, but equality a common pattern as well.

DV 5: Who can participate in collective religious ceremonies and rituals (excluding life-cycle ceremonies)?

	No. of cultures	%
1. Only males	4	6
2. Both, but males more commonly or more prominently, or some joint ceremonies, some solely male ceremonies, and no solely female ceremonies	36	49
3. Both, and fairly equal participation, although possibly with separation of the sexes	28	38
4. Both, but women more prominent, or some ceremonies for women, some joint, and none solely for men	5	7
5. No information, or no identifiable ceremonies	20	—
Total	93	100

We also included an item for the elaborateness of funeral ceremonies:

DV 6: Funeral or burial ceremonies held

	No. of cultures	%
1. Only for males, or for both, but more elaborate for males	11	13
2. For both, and roughly equal	73	87
3. No information	9	—
Total	93	100

55

In this latter item we note that there is very little variation, with funerals of equal elaborateness by far the predominant pattern. Several other items were excluded from our analysis because they showed even less deviation from this pattern of equality: birth ceremony elaborateness (only nine cases of male or female bias), birth ceremony participation (only four cases of exclusively male attendance), and prospects for an afterlife or reincarnation (only five cases of male bias). Comparing these instances of predominant equality with the pattern established for DV 1-DV 5, we note again that items dealing with larger collectivities and ceremonies show more male bias than those dealing with family events. In cultures around the world women may have status that is in various ways inferior to that of men, but in coming into and going out of this life the pattern of rituals seems almost everywhere to be one of equality.[2]

Two other religious items did not enter our analysis because they applied to only a few cultures, or because information on them could rarely be found: the possession of sacred objects restricted to one sex only (codable for only 25 out of 93 cultures) and ancestor worship (codable for only 27 cultures).

POLITICS

Three items were included in our coding form dealing with political leadership positions, covering the relative importance of men and women in positions spanning several communities, intermediate and local leadership positions (non-kin-group posts), and leadership of kin groups. It should be noted that in many of our sources we had to rely on the occasional mention of leaders at various levels, rather than on

2. The reader should keep in mind that our general coding rules specify to code for the ordinary population. In some cultures the male children of elites receive more elaborate birth ceremonies than daughters, and when male members of the elite die their funerals may be more elaborate than those of females. These cases merit secondary codes, but as long as the ordinary population did not show such a bias, a primary coding of rough equality was made.

56

a systematic listing of all past and present leaders and the norms governing whether and in what circumstances women might ascend to leadership posts. Therefore our codings may understate somewhat the ability of women to hold political posts in special circumstances. (On this general issue, see Lebeuf, 1963.) The intercommunity leadership item was omitted from our analysis because there were no such posts, or no information, for 45 out of our 93 cultures. The remaining two items both show a more pronounced male bias than any of our religious items.

DV 7: Intermediate or local political leaders (non-kin-group)

	No. of cultures	%
1. Only males	65	88
2. Both sexes, but male more numerous or more powerful or both	7	10
3. Both sexes, and males more numerous while women equally powerful or males more powerful while women are equally numerous	2	3
4. No such posts, or no information	19	—
Total	93	101

DV 8: Clearly defined leadership posts in kinship and/or extended family units

	No. of cultures	%
1. Include men only	52	84
2. Both, but men have more say and influence	6	10
3. Both, with roughly equal influence	4	6
4. No such posts, or no information	31	—
Total	93	100

These markedly skewed distributions accord with the common generalization (Tiger, 1969; Gough, 1972; Goldberg,

57

1973) that politics is the realm of social life that is most dominated by males. Lest we jump too quickly here to statements about universal male domination in politics, we should note that in spite of the strong male bias in these items there are nine or ten cultures in our sample where women do hold some political leadership positions, and that on the kin-group level there were four cultures where our coders judged that the influence of women leaders was equal to that of the men. The number of cases is small, but this is still a variation that merits examination.

We also included an item on participation of men and women in political gatherings and councils. However, since such gatherings were lacking or information unavailable in 36 out of our 93 cultures, this item has been omitted from subsequent analysis. However, we note that the distribution of the remaining cultures showed more male bias than our religious ceremony participation item (DV 5), with 29 cultures coded as having solely male participation (but with two cultures coded as having fully equal participation and voice for women).

A final political item concerned the participation of the sexes in warfare.

DV 9: In collective fighting and warfare, who participates?

	No. of cultures	%
1. Only males	62	89
2. Both, but men do most of the fighting, and women may aid	8	12
3. No warfare, or no information	23	—
Total	93	101

Here again we find a pattern of extreme male bias, but with women not completely excluded in every society. In general, then, our political items show a stronger male bias than the items on religion. In our sample, as in previous studies, there

58

were no cultures in which women were judged dominant or even somewhat more influential than men in either political leadership or warfare. Patterns of equality here are exceptions rather than one common pattern, as they were in the religious realm. Yet there are such exceptions.

ECONOMICS

Twelve separate items were used to construct a scale of the relative contribution of women to subsistence, following, with modifications, the procedures used earlier by Heath (1958) and Brown (1963). The main modification was to insert items dealing with crafts and manufacturing and with trade (earlier studies used only agriculture, herding and dairying, hunting and gathering, and fishing). In all cases the activities involved had to contribute to subsistence (defined as the provision of food, clothing, and shelter) in order to be coded, rather than simply having ceremonial or ornamental significance. The six different subsistence activities were coded on a 5-point scale from "insignificant, sporadic, or absent" to "the dominant subsistence activity." These were then converted into a 5-point scale with intervals of 15%, ranging from 0% up to 60%. Then there were another six items measuring the contribution of women relative to men for each type of subsistence activity (the criterion being the value of the contribution, rather than the amount of time and energy spent), each coded into five categories from solely male subsistence activity to solely female subsistence activity. These were then converted into five intervals of 25% each, ranging from 0% to 100% relative female contribution. The scale was then formed by multiplying the proportional contribution of women to each subsistence activity by the relative importance of that activity in a culture's overall subsistence. These quantities were summed and then divided by the total relative contributions of all activities to subsistence (This standardizes our results for the fact that some cultures may be coded as relying on only two or three of our six sub-

59

sistence activities, and others four, five, or even all six.) The results, which ranged in value from 0 to 1, were then divided into intervals of size .1. The final scale can be thought of roughly as a measure of the proportional contribution of women to subsistence, with intervals of 0-10%, 10-20%, 20-30%, etc. The final distribution appears as follows:

DV10 (IV 42): Proportional contribution of women to overall subsistence

	No. of cultures	%
1	2	2
2	2	2
3	14	15
4	23	25
5	27	30
6	18	20
7	2	2
8	4	4
9	0	0
10	0	0
Not ascertainable	1	—
Total	93	100

Here we note something closely approximating a normal (in the statistical sense, i.e., bell-shaped) distribution, with a slight tendency toward greater male than female contributions to subsistence cross-culturally.[3] This pattern can be

3. This distribution may understate the contributions women make to subsistence. The items upon which it is based required our coders to use the general information provided by ethnographers to assess both the relative importance of particular subsistence activities and the relative contribution of women to those activities. None of our ethnographies contained precise data, such as measures of the caloric value of the food items produced by men and by women. Recent research using such caloric measures often shows that women's subsistence contribution tends to get underestimated in ethnographers' eyes, since men's work may be more glamorous or arduous, even if less productive. In other words, cultural values and the differential

compared in a rough way with the findings, using slightly different procedures and different cross-cultural samples, of the earlier studies by Heath and Brown:

Heath (1957, p. 78)
Subsistence contribution of women

No. of cultures		%
0	23	6
1	34	9
2	74	19
3	90	23
4	71	18
5	56	14
6	33	8
7	13	3
8	4	1
9	0	0
10	0	0
Total	398	101

These distributions look similar to ours, with in each case a slight tendency for greater male contributions to be more common than greater female contributions cross-culturally. Heath's scale has more bias in this male direction than either our scale or Brown's, perhaps because he coded hunting, marine hunting, and the herding of large animals as exclusively male even when there was no specific information to that effect, while we did not. Our scale also has less variance

visibility of men's and women's work may produce a biased picture of how much of the total output is produced by women. Thus our scale may underestimate the relative subsistence contribution of women somewhat. However, we still expect this scale to be suitable for differentiating those cultures in which women do most of the subsistence work from those in which women play minimal subsistence roles. If the bias mentioned is fairly general, the differences between cultures with high and low scores on this scale should still reflect real differences in how much women contribute to subsistence.

Brown (1963, adapted from p. 848)
Relative contribution of women to subsistence

No. of cultures		%
1	6	8
2	9	12
3	7	9
4	19	25
5	10	13
6	13	17
7	5	7
8	5	7
9	1	1
10	0	0
Total	75	99

(dispersion from the mean) than either of the other two studies showed. Such small differences aside, the cross-cultural pattern approximates a statistically normal distribution, with more or less equal contributions by both sexes the most common pattern, but some cultures where women do more and a few more cultures where men do more. Clearly no conclusion that "women generally do most of the work" or that "men are generally the breadwinners" is justified by these figures.

A similar pattern emerges from a simple 3-point scale for the relative time and effort expended by men and women on subsistence activities (here it is the amount of work and not the output that is coded).

DV 11: Relative time and effort expended on subsistence activities

	No. of cultures	%
1. Men clearly expend more time and effort on subsistence	14	16
2. Men and women expend roughly equal time and effort	54	61

3. Women clearly expend more time and
effort on subsistence   20   23
4. Not ascertainable   5   —

| | Total | 93 | 100 |

Here there is a very slight tendency for harder work by women to be more common than harder work by men, but roughly equal efforts is much the most common pattern. In dependent variables 10 and 11 we see then a type of cross-cultural distribution we have not seen in previous items—neither the strong male bias of the political and leadership items nor the overwhelming equality of the birth and funeral items, but instead substantial variation around a modal pattern of nearly comparable male and female economic activity.

We also coded for the presence or absence of male and female collective work groups (the latter item was included in our discussion of independent variables in chapter III).

DV 12: Communitywide exclusively male work groups

	No. of cultures	%
1. None	20	26
2. One such activity	44	56
3. Two or more such activities	14	18
4. No information	15	—
Total	93	100

DV 13 (IV 41): Communitywide exclusively female work groups

	No. of cultures	%
1. None	45	63
2. One or more such activity	27	38
3. No information	21	—
Total	93	101

63

Our figures are not too different from those found in an earlier cross-cultural study by Young (1965). He found collective male subsistence activity present in 31 out of his 54 cultures and collective female subsistence activity present in 10 (compared with 58 and 27 out of 93 cultures in our sample). The generalization that collective male work groups are more common than collective female work groups cross-culturally is confirmed (see also Tiger, 1969), but almost one-third of the cultures in our sample do have such female groups.

We also included an item dealing with the stringency with which men and women keep apart from each other when performing any subsistence activities to which both sexes contribute. (I.e., sharp segregation was not coded here for activities performed solely by men or solely by women, but only for activities engaged in by both sexes.)

DV 14: In all subsistence activities in which both men and women participate, code whether:

	No. of cultures	%
1. Men and women are sharply segregated	15	20
2. Some segregation, or segregation in some of these activities	41	53
3. Little or no segregation in these activities	21	27
4. No information	16	—
Total	93	100

Here we see a normal distribution again, with partial segregation the most common pattern.

Our coding form included four items dealing with property rights: private property rights in items of some economic value, individual rights of use of collectively owned property, rights of disposal of property, and inheritance rights. Unfortunately the people living in many of the cultures

64

in our sample don't make such neat legalistic distinctions, or our sources failed to report them. As a result, the coders on our project had considerable difficulty agreeing on the codings of these four items, and only the inheritance item surpassed the arbitrary minimum intercoder agreement score we established (70% initial agreement). Only this final item on inheritance rights, for which there was initial intercoder agreement in 73% of the cultures in our sample, entered the pool of dependent variable items we will be using in subsequent analysis.[4] The other three items did show a cross-cultural distribution similar to that given below for inheritance rights, with a range from exclusive male rights to equality in rights, with only one to five cultures coded as giving some general preference to women. We also included a separate item for dwelling ownership, and here there is less marked bias in favor of men.

DV 15 (IV 40): Who can inherit property of some economic value?

	No. of cultures	%
1. Only males, or males except in unusual circumstances	18	25
2. Both, but males have definite preference in inheritance	27	38
3. Roughly equal inheritance rights by sex	22	31
4. Female preference, or exclusive female rights	4	6
5. No such property, or no information	22	—
Total	93	100

4. The first of these four items, concerning individual property rights, was recoded for use as an independent variable (IV 28), dealing with the existence or nonexistence of private property. Since the intercoder disagreements referred more to whether men or women had such rights rather than whether private property existed in the first place, it was felt acceptable to use the item in this collapsed form.

65

DV 16:   Who owns or controls the use of the dwellings?

	No. of cultures	%
1. Owned or controlled solely by men	22	31
2. Most owned by men, some by women	12	17
3. Equal ownership, or no preferential rights	25	35
4. Most or all owned or controlled by women	13	18
5. No information	21	—
Total	93	101

In this study we distinguished property rights from control over the results of the labor of men and women, and we included three separate items (already noted in chapter III as independent variables) for the control of the fruits of male, female, and joint labor:[5]

DV 17 (IV 43):   Who controls the disposal and use of the fruits of the labor done only by men?

	No. of cultures	%
1. Men have virtually total say	30	33
2. Men have the predominant say, or no indication of preference	41	45
3. Men and women have equal say	12	13
4. Women have the predominant or total say	9	10
5. No such fruits	1	—
Total	93	101

5. In the initial recoding the code of "ambiguous" was, following the common procedure, collapsed with the modal (i.e., most commonly occurring) category in these three items, and that is the meaning of the term "no indication of preference" that occurs

DV 18 (IV 44): Who controls the disposal and use of the fruits of the joint labor of men and women?

	No. of cultures	%
1. Men have virtually total say	7	9
2. Men have the predominant say	6	7
3. Men and women have equal say, or no indication of preference	60	74
4. Women have the predominant or total say	8	10
5. No such fruits	12	—
Total	93	100

DV 19 (IV 45): Who controls the disposal and use of the fruits of the labor done only by women?

	No. of cultures	%
1. Men have virtually total say or predominant say	7	8
2. Men and women have equal say	9	10
3. Women have the predominant say, or no indication of preference	62	67
4. Women have virtually total say	14	15
5. No such fruits	1	—
Total	93	100

We see here a fairly normal distribution on the item dealing with the joint labor of men and women, but with each sex tending to monopolize control over the fruits of the labor

grouped with a different phrase in each of the three items above. This grouping procedure tends to obscure the meaning of the categories somewhat, and in retrospect it might have been better simply to leave these cases as a separate category, to be coded as a blank for subsequent statistical computations.

done only by that sex. However, even on these items there exist a few cultures in which one sex controls the fruits of the labor done by the opposite sex.

We also included an item on male contributions to household work (defined as cooking, clothes making, and child care).[6] Here we found not unexpectedly that there were no cultures with either equal or predominant contributions by men. This accords with the common generalization that, while work outside the home tends to vary widely from one culture to another, throughout the world work within the home tends to be predominantly done by women (cf. Stephens, 1963, pp. 278-284).

DV 20: Who does the domestic work?

	No. of cultures	%
1. Males do virtually none	47	51
2. Males do some, but mostly done by females	45	49
3. Contributions equal, or mostly done by males	0	0
4. No information	1	—
Total	93	100

In general then for our economic items, with the exception of this coding for domestic work, the distribution within our sample tends to be either relatively equal (in terms of male or female bias) or to reflect some male bias, but with numerous exceptions. Also, the items dealing with contributions to the economy tend to be more equally distributed than those dealing with rights and control over economic goods.

6. It should be noted that clothes making, while included here as part of domestic work, was also coded as a subsistence activity in DV 10, as part of handicraft and manufacturing activity. Food preparation and child care were not classified as subsistence activities for DV 10.

Sexual and Family Life

We coded for the presence or absence of a premarital and extramarital sexual double standard, and for the extent to which married women could and did engage in extramarital affairs. The results are as follows:

DV 21: Is there a sexual double standard in regard to premarital sex?

	No. of cultures	%
1. Yes	32	44
2. No, equal restrictions	41	56
3. Does not apply, or no information	20	—
Total	93	100

DV 22: Is there an extramarital double standard?

	No. of cultures	%
1. Yes	32	43
2. No, equal restrictions	41	55
3. Yes, but it favors females	2	3
4. No information	18	—
Total	93	101

DV 23: Are married women allowed to, and do they in fact, have extramarital affairs?

	No. of cultures	%
1. Not allowed, and apparently rare	40	47
2. Not allowed, but apparently not uncommon	29	34
3. Allowed, or very common	17	20
4. No information	7	—
Total	93	101

69

Here the first two items fit the common observation that sexual restrictions often fall more heavily on women than on men. In both cases equal restrictions is the most common pattern, but a double standard favoring males is also very common. The two cultures for which we coded an extramarital double standard favoring females (Gilbertese and Gilyak) are both cases in which adultery is forbidden to both, but when caught in the act the male is subject to a more severe penalty than the female. These two cultures refute the statement made by Goldberg (1973, p. 179) that "there is no society that is not more lenient with the adulterous male than with the adulterous female." (Actually our 41 cultures without an extramarital double standard destroy this generalization as well.) The final item, in addition to giving us a scale of the relative strictness of prevention of the extramarital affairs of women, shows a figure of 69 out of 93 cultures with some sort of rule against adultery, or 74%. This figure sandwiches in nicely between the figures given in two previous cross-cultural studies, 61% (Ford and Beach, 1951, p. 115) and 82% (Murdock, 1949, p. 265).

We also created a scale for the severity of menstrual taboos, using roughly the procedures devised by Stephens (1962, pp. 206-212) and Young and Bacdayan (1965). The result is a 7-step menstrual taboo scale (see the discussion in chapter III of Guttman scaling). The coefficient of scalability is an acceptable .72, although for this scale we reach our self-imposed maximum of 31 cultures for which no information is given.

DV 24: What menstrual restrictions and taboos are present?

	No. of cultures	%
1. No menstrual taboos	10	16
2. Rule versus intercourse with menstruating women	15	24

3. +Personal restriction on menstruants,
   e.g., dietary   9   15
4. +Stated belief that menstrual blood
   is dangerous to men   3   5
5. +A rule that menstruating women
   may not cook for men   3   5
6. +Menstruating women are segregated
   from men, perhaps in a menstrual hut   6   10
7. +A rule that menstruating women
   may not have contact with some male
   things, e.g., bow, fishing gear, etc.   16   26
8. No information   31   —

                                     Total   93   101

This item includes combinations of traits used by both Stephens and by Young and Bacdayan, which makes comparisons difficult. In retrospect it would have been wiser to collapse some of the intermediate scale steps, since they differentiate few cases. (Stephens followed this procedure and ended up using a 4-point scale in later work.) Unlike the results in Young and Bacdayan's study, in our sample the item about female contact with male gear scaled "higher" than the item for seclusion in menstrual huts. However, this difference is not significant, since in most of our cultures these two traits occur together, and scaling them in the order we have them result in only slightly fewer errors in scaling than when they are included in the reverse order.

Items were included in our coding form to tap both beliefs about the relative roles of the sexes in procreation and relative sexual drives.

DV 25:   How is the role of men and women in procreation understood?

                                               No. of
                                               cultures   %
1. Men are thought to play the most important role   7   8

                                                              71

2. Belief in roughly equal contributions
or no evidence of greater contribution
by either sex   81   87
3. Women are thought to play the most
important role   5   5
                                                             ___   ___
                                              Total   93   100

DV 26:   How are sexual drives and urges understood?

	No. of cultures	%
1. Men are thought to have stronger urges	17	18
2. Belief that urges are roughly equal or no evidence of belief in greater urges for either sex	72	77
3. Women are thought to have stronger urges	4	4
Total	93	99

The first item shows that cultures that view one sex or the
other as largely peripheral to the act of procreation are in a
decided minority, even though nineteenth-century evolutionists and some modern-day feminists (e.g., Millett, 1969, pp.
111-116) have gotten much theoretical mileage out of positing
a general stage of ignorance of paternity in the evolution of
humanity. Although we can't tell yet how this item involving
knowledge of paternity is related to other aspects of the
status of women, there do seem to exist many contemporary
simple societies that acknowledge the role of the male, and
even some that believe that the role of the male in procreation is greater than that of the female.

The pattern discovered for sexual drives corresponds
roughly to the generalizations made by Ford and Beach
1951 (pp. 101-102) about initiative in sexual advances.
They found that in most of the societies in their cross-culture
sample men were supposed to take the initiative in making
sexual advances, but that in practice in the majority of socie-

ties the women also actively sought sexual liaisons. In fact in a minority of societies women were supposed to begin all love affairs. In summarizing the evidence from higher animal species and humans, they state (p. 101): "There is a widespread belief that male animals of most species always assume complete command of the mating situation and inevitably play the more active role in precoital courtship. Nothing could be further from the truth. Distribution of initiative varies from species to species, but in the main the relationship is a reciprocal one in which both partners are sexually aggressive and each contributes to the complete arousal of the other."

The pattern we find leads us to disagree fundamentally with the conclusion Nimkoff reached based on the cross-cultural distribution of different marriage systems (Nimkoff, 1965, p. 17): "In a world sample of 554 societies, polygyny was culturally favored in 415; monogamy in 135; and polyandry in 4. These figures . . . buttress the thesis that men are generally governed by sexual drives and are disposed toward sexual variety much more than are women." Our direct coding for beliefs about sexual drives fails to show anything like this skewed distribution, and we are led to conclude that other factors must be behind the commonness of polygyny and the rarity of polyandry.

We also included an item for whether sexual activity was viewed as dangerous or contaminating. The following distribution resulted:

DV 27: Is there an explicit view that sexual activity is dangerous or contaminating in some way?

	No. of cultures	%
1. Yes	15	22
2. No	53	78
3. No information	25	—
Total	93	100

73

Generally the coding of yes reflects a belief in the danger of sexual activity to men (rather than to women or to both), which leads to various kinds of purification and abstention rituals.

Items dealing with both the role of elders in marriage arrangements and the role of the potential bride and groom commonly show a pattern of equality, but with more cases of greater male say than greater female say.

DV 28:   Role of the older generation in arranging marriages (first marriages only)

	No. of cultures	%
1. Males monopolize arrangements completely	13	16
2. Both males and females participate, but males have more say.	32	39
3. Both males and females participate roughly equally	29	35
4. Both males and females, but females have more say	9	11
5. No information, does not apply	10	—
Total	93	101

DV 29:   Voice of the potential bride and groom in marriages (first marriages)

	No. of cultures	%
1. Only the potential groom can initiate or refuse a match	4	5
2. Groom has more authority than bride to initiate or refuse	27	34
3. Equal authority to initiate or refuse a match	46	58
4. Bride has more authority than groom to initiate or refuse	3	4
5. No information	13	—
Total	93	101

Items dealing with marriage finance and ideal marriage forms follow patterns similar to those shown in earlier cross-cultural work done by Murdock and others, with bride price the most common form of marriage finance and polygyny much more common than polyandry (see the figures cited by Nimkoff above, which stem from Murdock's work).[7]

DV 30: What kind of marriage payments are made? (first marriage)

	No. of cultures	%
1. Woman exchange	5	7
2. Substantial bride price	36	47
3. Bride service	10	13
4. Token bride price	10	13
5. Gift exchange	10	13
6. Dowry	6	8
7. No information	16	—
Total	93	101

DV 31 (IV 46): Preferred marriage forms

	No. of cultures	%
1. General polygyny (polygynous unions over 20% of all unions)	22	24
2. Limited polygyny (favored, but under 20% of all unions)	35	38
3. Monogamy—plural marriages either forbidden or nonpreferential and infrequent	34	37
4. Polyandry	2	2
Total	93	101

7. In DV 30 woman exchange is ordered above substantial bride price on the suggestion of Schlegel, 1972, p. 21, that woman exchange should be considered the highest form of bride price.

DV 32: Are multiple spouses allowed?

	No. of cultures	%
1. Only for males	71	77
2. For both, but more commonly for males	4	4
3. For neither	15	16
4. For both, but more commonly for females	2	2
5. No information	1	—
Total	93	99

Our proportion of 2 out of 93 cultures preferring polyandry is of course higher than the 4 out of 554 cited by Nimkoff, which stems from the original figures in Murdock, 1957. No doubt this higher percentage is due to the fact that Murdock and White used cultural distinctiveness as one of the criteria for picking cultures for their standard cross-cultural sample, and societies practicing polyandry are decidedly distinctive. Note also that our second marriage item reveals that neither of these two cultures prohibits polygyny, and that there are four additional societies in our sample in which polygyny is favored, but women having more than one husband is also allowed.

We also coded for the presence or absence of a custom called the *levirate*, which means that when a man dies his wife should be remarried to his brother or to some other male kinsman. We included this item in our dependent variable pool because Young and Bacdayan (1965) used it as one item in a scale of "male dominance" they devised.

DV 33: Levirate

	No. of cultures	%
1. Present	54	71
2. Absent	22	29
3. No information	17	—
Total	93	100

Murdock in his early cross-cultural sample of 249 cultures (1949, p. 29) found the levirate present in preferential form in 126 societies, absent or merely occasional in 58, with no information available on 65. In percentage terms these figures correspond quite closely to ours.

We also added an item having to do with which spouse has to move farther from the natal home at the time of marriage. Here we think of this as an aspect of the relative power of the two sexes, although this item is, of course, closely related to the residence rules in a given society, which we have thought of earlier as an independent variable.

DV 34: What are the relative distances moved by bride and groom away from their families of orientation at first marriage?

	No. of cultures	%
1. The female generally moves farther away	58	69
2. Generally about equal distances	7	8
3. The male generally moves farther away	19	23
4. No information	9	—
Total	93	100

The resulting distribution does, in fact, correspond closely to our coding for residence rules, in which there were 18 cultures having preferential matrilocal postmarital residence.

We also coded for the relative ease of men and women in initiating divorce and in remarrying after the death or divorce of a spouse.

DV 35: What is the relative ease of divorce (initiating divorce)?

	No. of cultures	%
1. Divorce is in theory only available to men	5	5
2. Divorce is possible for both, but more difficult for women	12	13

77

3. Divorce is equally possible for both, no indication of bias	72	77
4. Divorce is possible for both, but more difficult for men, or in theory only available for women	4	4
Total	93	99

DV 36:   What is the relative ease of remarriage?

	No. of cultures	%
1. Possible for both, but less obstacles for men	21	25
2. Equally possible for both men and women	64	75
3. No information	8	—
Total	93	100

In regard to the question of divorce rights, we note some disagreement in the existing literature. Most early cross-cultural surveys concluded that divorce was easier in many cultures for men than for women (e.g., Hobhouse, Wheeler, and Ginsberg, 1915, p. 164), but Murdock (1950) found that divorce was generally equally accessible to both sexes. (Minturn, Grosse, and Haider, 1966, concluded from their cross-cultural sample that there was not enough information on the divorce rights of women to make such a judgment.) We find equal divorce rights by far the most common pattern, but with exceptions in both directions, with greater male rights somewhat more common than greater female rights. This pattern is even more marked on the remarriage item, where there were no cultures coded as making it easier for women than men to remarry. It should be noted that the 21 cultures we coded as making remarriage more difficult for females are in some cases cultures where the levirate is a prescription rather than simply a preference. In such a culture the greater obstacles faced by the woman refer primarily to the strict control her deceased husband's kinsmen have over her remarriage choice, rather than to an inability to remarry at all.

We also coded for the relative ages of men and women at first marriage, although we were not at all certain that this had much to do with the status of women.

DV 37:   What is the average relative age at first marriage of men and of women?[8]

	No. of cultures	%
1. Women generally older	2	3
2. Ages about equal	7	10
3. Men 1–2 years older	12	17
4. Men 3–4 years older	18	26
5. Men more than 4 years older	31	44
6. No information	23	—
Total	93	100

This pattern fits the general observation (cf. Stephens, 1963, p. 392) that in most societies men are older than women at first marriage, a fact various authors have attributed to earlier sexual maturation of females, widespread polygyny, and the custom of the bride price (the latter two customs cause males to marry late by producing a shortage of females and by requiring a period of work and saving by men in order to finance their marriages). Note, however, that there are a minority of cultures coded as exceptions to this pattern, including two cultures (Atayal and Trumai) we have coded as having women marrying somewhat later than men. Thus whatever the powerful social and biological factors are that lead men to marry at a later age than women

8. These figures refer to the relative ages in society in general at which women first marry and at which men first marry, rather than the average age gap between couples at marriage. In cultures with substantial polygyny the two figures can be different.

in most societies, in some circumstances these factors can be overridden.

Two items were included having to do with final authority over infants and children.

DV 38: Who has final authority over the care, handling and discipline of infant children (up to 3-4 years old)?

	No. of cultures	%
1. Final authority is monopolized by males, or males have more say	12	18
2. Final authority is divided roughly equally	11	16
3. Final authority is divided, but females have more say	21	31
4. Final authority is monopolized by females	23	34
5. No information	26	—
Total	93	99

DV 39: Who has final authority over the upbringing and discipline of postinfant unmarried children living in the home?

	No. of cultures	%
1. Final authority is virtually monopolized by males	11	16
2. Final authority is divided, but males have more say	14	21
3. Final authority is divided roughly equally	34	50
4. Authority is divided and females have more say, or final say is virtually monopolized by females	9	13
5. No information	25	—
Total	93	100

80

For the item dealing with infants we get, as we might expect, one of our few cases of a strong bias in the favor of women. For the item dealing with children we get a distribution that is more nearly normal (i.e., bell-shaped), but with a skew in the other direction, toward male dominance. In both items, though, there are a fair number of cases coded as exceptions to these patterns.

We also constructed a Guttman scale of deference of wives to husbands, following roughly the procedure of Stephens (1963). We got the following distribution:

DV 40:   Wife to husband institutionalized deference.

	No. of cultures	%
1. None of the following coded	29	35
2. Husband dominates decision making	15	18
3. +Wife excluded from many social gatherings	21	25
4. +Wife rarely disputes husband	9	11
5. +Husband has seating priority	7	8
6. +Wife kneels or bows when greeting husband	3	4
7. No information	9	—
Total	93	101

This scale has a coefficient of scalability of .69, which is just above the generally accepted minimum.[9] Cultures range

9. The ordering of the items for our deference scale is quite different from that found by Stephens (who got the above items to scale in the order 1,3,5,2,4,6). Stephens does not give the coefficient of scalability for his wife-to-husband deference scale, but he does say (p. 423) that this scale is not as good as the other Guttman scales he constructed in the same study. We can use our scale as a measure of the relative strength of wife-to-husband deference in our sample, but the very different ordering of scale steps in comparison with the results of Stephens leads us to doubt that either order is a strong cross-cultural regularity. We did find, with Stephens, that wife-to-husband deference was much more common than husband-to-wife

from a large minority with no visible signs of deference through a few with many different signs.

Items were also included dealing with preference for male or female children and for the relative incidence of infanticide. For both items the pattern is most commonly one of equality, but with some male bias:

DV 41:   Is there a stated preference for children of one sex?

	No. of cultures	%
1. For males	28	30
2. Equal, no preference	54	58
3. For females	11	12
Total	93	100

DV 42:   Is there any evidence of infanticide?

	No. of cultures	%
1. Mostly for females	6	9
2. For both, or for neither	64	90
3. Mostly for males	1	1
4. No information	22	—
Total	93	100

Note that item DV 41 shows that the large majority of our cultures are exceptions to the statement frequently made

deference. Thirty-one cultures were coded as having some sort of husband-to-wife institutionalized deference (compared with 55 cultures with wife-to-husband deference), but most of these were cases of husbands not using the personal name of the wife. This turned out to be generally a reciprocal custom, with the wife not using the personal name of the husband in the same cultures. As such this custom cannot be considered as an indication of deference in one direction, and the custom of wives not using the personal names of their husbands failed to scale with the other customs in DV 40.

that people in most societies prefer to have sons rather than daughters.

Also included were items on the relative age of beginning training for adult duties for boys and girls and the relative punishment applied for misbehavior. As explained in appendix 1, we had originally wanted to include other items dealing with the differential socialization of boys and girls, but in a pretest we found that information on more subtle differences in this area was lacking in most ethnographic sources.

DV 43: Are boys or girls trained earlier for adult duties?

	No. of cultures	%
1. Boys are trained earlier generally	1	1
2. Training begins at roughly equal ages, or no stated bias	70	75
3. Girls are trained earlier generally	22	24
Total	93	100

DV 44: Are boys or girls punished more severely for equal misbehavior?

	No. of cultures	%
1. Boys are punished more severely	3	3
2. Punishment about equal, no stated bias	82	88
3. Girls are punished more severely	8	9
Total	93	100

In both of these items the pattern again is one of predominant equality, but with a slight skew in the direction of punishing girls more severely, and a more marked bias toward earlier training of girls. Again the status implication of these items is not immediately obvious, since we could think of high status as indicated by either the earlier assumption of adult duties or by the freedom to continue games and childish pastimes.

To conclude this section on sexual and family life items we have two variables dealing with the use of force and the general dominance of husbands relative to wives (and vice versa).

DV 45:   Is physical punishment of the spouse condoned?

	No. of cultures	%
1. Only husband hitting wife, generally	39	62
2. Physical punishment by neither	16	25
3. Either may hit the other, or only wife may hit husband	8	13
4. No information	30	—
Total	93	100

DV 46:   Is there an explicit view that men should and do dominate their wives?

	No. of cultures	%
1. Yes	42	67
2. No, evidence of rough equality	19	30
3. No, evidence of general wife dominance	2	3
4. No information	30	—
Total	93	100

In both of these items there is much more evidence of male bias, although again there are exceptions. Equality is a not infrequent pattern, and there are even two cultures for DV 46 (Javanese and Bribri) for which wife domination was coded. We will want to return to a further examination of this last item in the concluding pages of this chapter.

In the preceding section we have examined items dealing

with the relative status of women in sexual and family life, and these items fail to follow any single pattern. They range all the way from variables showing strong male bias (e.g., having multiple spouses), through fairly equal distributions of various types (the role of the sexes in procreation, authority over children) to items showing female predominance (authority over infants). There are some general patterns (for example, greater control over female sexual activity is not uncommon cross-culturally, while greater control over male sexual activity is rare or nonexistent), but otherwise summary statements are difficult.

MISCELLANEOUS

We coded for the participation of women relative to men in general community meetings, activities, and organizations. Here the pattern ranges from equality to male dominance, with no cultures coded as having females dominant in these domains. The distribution is similar to, although perhaps with slightly more male bias than, our earlier item for participation in community religious ceremonials (DV 5).

DV 47: In general community gatherings, activities, and organizations, who can attend and participate (exclude religious and political gatherings already dealt with)?

	No. of cultures	%
1. Only men, or both, but men more often or more prominently	27	44
2. Both equally, although perhaps segregated	35	57
3. No information	31	—
Total	93	101

85

We also formed a Guttman scale of female initiation rites, although again we were not clear that these customs had any obvious connection with the general status of women. Some people have seen female initiation rites as indicating the special status and importance of women, while others have felt that they indicate the subjugation of women (especially where these rituals involve operations or punishment, even though these are generally administered by other women, not by men). We followed the procedures indicated by Young (1965, p. 15) and got the following Guttman scale pattern:

DV 48: Existence of general female initiation ceremonies.

	No. of cultures	%
1. No initations for females	36	47
2. Customary minimal social recognition	8	11
3. +Personal dramatization of the initiate	10	13
4. +Organized social response	12	16
5. +Affective social response (e.g., punishment or operations)	10	13
6. No information	17	—
Total	93	100

The coefficient of scalability of this scale is .92, and here the items and item order are the same as those found by Young. Thus the logic of an underlying continuum of elaborateness of initiation ceremonies cross-culturally is strongly supported. We also note that our figure of 36 out of 93 societies lacking female initiation is not far different from Young's figure of 42% for societies lacking female initiation ceremonies in his sample (p. 14).

We also included an item on the presence or absence of myths or historical tales about women having had loftier status in ages past. This was included largely because theorists of matriarchy (e.g., Bachofen, 1861; Davis, 1971), claim

86

that such myths are very common and are indicative of a previous historical stage when women dominated social life.

DV 49:   Is there in folklore or history any belief that the status of women has changed?

	No. of cultures	%
1. A belief it has declined	6	7
2. No such belief, no change	83	89
3. A belief it has improved	4	4
Total	93	100

Our sample gives no evidence that there is such a widespread belief cross-culturally in a former "golden age" for women. (Even where category 1 was coded, it generally referred not to some prior golden age when women ruled men, but to a change in the status of women from bad to worse.)

Three final items attempt to get at generalized notions of the relations between the sexes. We included an item designed to tap "machismo," since some writers see men's obsession with aggression and sexual conquest as the main source of the low status of women.

DV 50:   Is there a general high value placed on males being aggressive, strong, and sexually potent?

	No. of cultures	%
1. Marked emphasis	26	32
2. Moderate emphasis	33	41
3. Little or no emphasis	22	27
4. Ambiguous	12	—
Total	93	100

We also asked whether there was a clearly stated belief that women are generally inferior to men (inferior in several different ways, and for all women). That item showed the following distribution:

87

DV 51:   Is there a clearly stated belief that women are generally inferior to men?

	No. of cultures	%
1. Yes	27	29
2. No such belief	66	71
3. Belief that women are superior in general	0	0
Total	93	100

Here we see a by now familiar pattern of equality the general pattern, but male bias also common. There are no cases at all of female bias.

Finally, we included an item dealing with the informal influence of women. This was included as at least a partial check on the tendency of some ethnographic studies and cross-cultural codes to focus on the ideal and formalized aspects of cultures, and to miss the informal and behind-the-scenes aspects where many commentators have seen substantial female power lodged (see the discussion in chapter II). In fact we find that women in almost half of the cultures have at least somewhat more informal influence than the formal rules of the culture make it appear.

DV 52:   Does the ethnographer(s) say that women have more informal influence than the formal norms of the society would make it appear?

	No. of cultures	%
1. No such statement or implication	49	53
2. A statement or implication that they have somewhat more influence	25	27
3. A statement or implication that they have much more informal influence	19	20
Total	93	100

CONCLUSIONS

What have we learned from this survey of the distribution of our 93 cultures across so many variables? Before attempting to generalize we should caution that the overall pattern is a reflection of the particular items used, and even of the wording of the categories within them. While we think we have included here items from broad realms of social life, worded so as to detect high as well as low status of women, no arbitrary listing of items can be perfect. Also, whether the patterns revealed seem novel depends on the reader's expectations, and if the conceptions readers have of the status of the sexes around the world are anywhere near as diverse as those in the available literature, reactions are bound to differ. Given these qualifications, several generalizations seem in order.

First, it should be clear that equality and male bias are the most common patterns. Items skewed in favor of females are few and predictable (control over the fruits of female labor, authority over infants, domestic labor), and there are many items for which few or no cultures at all are coded as favoring women (e.g., community participation, marriage forms, premarital sexual restrictions). Even the exceptions to this pattern, where a few cultures show a female bias on an item while most cultures show a male bias, tend to be different cultures in each case. These findings fit the generalization accepted by most anthropologists that there are no known cultures in which women are generally dominant over men, whereas there are quite a few in which the reverse is true (see Lowie, 1920, chapter 8; Gough, 1972, p. 115).

At the same time these data do show many areas of substantial equality between the sexes. In areas such as subsistence work, funeral ceremonies, sexual drives, and access to divorce the most common pattern is one of equality, and no statement about the general dominance of men can hold

89

up. Even for some variables that do show clear biases in favor of men (e.g., control over the fruits of male labor, the role of elders in marriage arrangement, child preference) there is a sizable minority of cultures in which the opposite tendency of a bias in favor of women exists.

At this point we take issue with a recent work dealing with our topic. Steven Goldberg contends in his recent book, *The Inevitability of Patriarchy* (1973), that there are three cross-cultural universals favoring men: patriarchy (which he defines as a system of organization that associates authority and leadership primarily with males and in which males fill the vast majority of leadership positions), male dominance (which he defines as a societal feeling that the woman's will is somehow subordinated to the male's and that general authority in dyadic and family relationships ultimately resides in the male), and a tendency for males to monopolize whatever high status nonmaternal roles and tasks exist in a given society. He argues that these three universals are the result of hormonal differences between the sexes, which lead men to be more aggressive than women in every society and to strive for these three kinds of dominance over women. Goldberg is asserting universals rather than acknowledging variations, and he admits that the discovery of even one society that does not exhibit patriarchy, male dominance, and male monopolization of high-status nonmaternal roles will destroy his theory. The evidence we have presented in the preceding pages shows a number of exceptions, at least on the final two universals.

Our study includes few items dealing with leadership outside of the family, particularly since two items on our original coding form, one dealing with the highest political leadership posts and another dealing with economic leadership posts, were not codable for most societies. This leaves us with two variables, DV 7 (dealing with intermediate and local leadership posts) and DV 8 (dealing with kin-group and extended-family leadership posts). We saw earlier that both of these variables were highly skewed in favor of men, supporting the

90

general thrust of Goldberg's remarks on patriarchy. Variable DV 7 does, however, show two cultures (Bemba and Saramacca) coded as having either women leaders with power equal to male leaders at the same level, while less numerous, or such women leaders present in equal numbers but with less power. Variable DV 8 shows four cultures (Nubians, Semang, Iban, and Marquesans) in which women have equal influence with males in kin-group leadership. In no case do we get any codings of female dominance on these items, but these six exceptions to the pattern of male bias lead us to suspect that Goldberg may have overstated the case even for patriarchy. These are cultures that have leadership posts outside of the immediate family from which women are not as excluded as Goldberg's study would lead us to expect.

For male dominance the evidence is clearer. There are a number of variables described in this chapter that deal with authority and power within the family: DV 28, DV 38, DV 39, DV 40, and DV 46. In our sample we find 9 cultures in which women of the older generation have more say than men in arranging marriages, 23 cultures in which final authority over infants is monopolized by women, 9 cultures in which final authority over children is in the hands of women, or women have more say than men, 29 cultures in which none of five common kinds of deference to husbands could be found, and 21 cultures lacking an explicit view that men should and do dominate their wives, including two cultures in which, in practice, the wives dominate their husbands.[10]

10. One of these two cultures, the Javanese as studied by Hildred Geertz (see appendix 2), is one of the "frequently cited exceptions to male dominance" that Goldberg tries to refute (pp. 242-243). The case is somewhat ambiguous. The husband does seem to have a certain formal status within the family, but he is at the same time somehow relatively uninvolved in most aspects of the management of family affairs. Based on the descriptions of Geertz, the Javanese wife's authority does not extend merely to certain matters concerning the home and children as Goldberg implies (p. 40), but includes as well areas such as family economic management and marketing. The de facto authority of women in the home is such that they do not seem

Goldberg is sometimes inconsistent in whether by male dominance he means that societies feel men should dominate their wives (his stated definition) or whether they actually do so. Both the ideal and the actuality are dealt with in our items, and we find instead of universal male dominance a pattern of frequent exceptions. Male dominance is perhaps the most common pattern cross-culturally, and it could probably be argued that there is no culture in our sample in which there is a general feeling that a man's will should be subordinated to his wife's, i.e., no cases of clear female dominance, as defined by Goldberg. However, there does seem to be a significant minority of cultures in which general authority in dyadic and family relations is relatively equal. These cases disprove the universality of male dominance just as much as cultures showing female dominance would.

We have less evidence from our study on the issue of male monopolization of extrafamilial high-status roles, but it seems just as conclusive. Besides the two items for political leadership posts already mentioned (DV 7 and DV 8) we have only one item to rely on, DV 3, the sex of shamans. Here we have coded seven cultures in which women shamans are either more numerous or more powerful than men shamans or both, including two cultures (Abkhaz and Atayal) with only female shamans. With the role of the shaman, at least, universal monopolization by males is refuted. In Goldberg's book he dismisses similar troublesome cases, such as the predominance of women doctors in the Soviet Union, by saying that in such cases the role in question is not a high-status one (p. 171). Yet there is an element of circularity in

---

to have to use their feminine wiles to "get around" their husbands as Goldberg says they should where male dominance is present. Goldberg's dealing with such cases that appear to deviate from his argument shows that he can always find some statement in the existing sources that seems to imply some aspect of male dominance, but he does not convincingly show that general male dominance as he defines it exists in every society.

his reasoning. Men monopolize high-status roles, therefore if there is a role predominantly occupied by women it must have low status otherwise men would monopolize it. In the case of Soviet doctors he states that the status of doctors in the USSR is lower than in the United States. The status of Soviet doctors may not be as exalted relative to other occupations as in America, but it is still a relatively high-status occupation, one that is sought after ahead of many lower-status jobs (factory, clerical, sales, and service work), some of which are monopolized by men. In our study we lack a ranking of shamans relative to other specialized roles, and we can only state that the role of the shaman is generally one of some prestige and influence that sets the occupant off in a positive way from those who lack the required skills or gifts. Cross-culturally, as we noted earlier, there is a tendency for men to monopolize the shaman role more often than women, but again cultures in which there is a fairly equal distribution and even female predominance also exist.

Thus our data lead us to doubt all three of Goldberg's universals, and our doubts are strongest in the case of male dominance. Perhaps Goldberg would have been on safe ground if he had stated that no cultures exist that show what he would call matriarchy, female dominance, and monopolization by women of all high-status nonmaternal roles and tasks. However, it is not correct to state that all cultures are patriarchies with male dominance and male monopolization of such high-status roles. Rather there is a pattern of variation cross-culturally that includes cultures in which some or all of these three features of social organization are equal or even biased toward women. By trying to prove the existence of universals, Goldberg has been led to ignore the damage that cultures with aspects of equality and limited kinds of bias in favor of women (rather than a general bias in favor of females) do to his argument. There may never have been a society of Amazons ruling men, but our approach, which involves examining existing cross-cultural variations, shows

93

that cultures do exist that do not fit the asserted universal patterns of patriarchy, male dominance, and monopolization of high-status roles by men.

The patterns shown in this chapter do have parallels at a number of points with the findings of earlier research based on very different cross-cultural samples, although there are occasional conflicts as well. We cannot yet be certain whether all the traits listed in this chapter have the status implications we might suppose, but a picture of considerable complexity is emerging. On the basis of these frequency distributions alone it is clear that various aspects of what we have supposed to be a general concept, the relative status of women, are distributed in a number of different ways across our sample. Already we can see that if we wish to make cross-cultural generalizations about the status of women relative to men, we will have to be much more specific than some previous scholars in stating precisely what aspects of the relative status of women we are talking about. Political leadership is highly skewed in favor of males, shamanism less so; polyandry does seem almost as rare as previous work has indicated, beliefs in stronger male sex drives do not seem to be as common as some have supposed.

By looking only at the distribution of these individual variables, however, we get only half of the picture of how the status of women varies cross-culturally. Does male political dominance tend to occur together with sexual double standards favoring males? Or with predominant male property rights, or strict menstrual taboos? Without examining the pattern of associations among our 52 dependent variables we cannot answer such questions. This is the task of the next chapter.

CHAPTER V

The Status of Women:
One Phenomenon or Many?

Now that we have looked at both our hypotheses and our
dependent variables, the next step is to examine the inter-
relations within the dependent variable pool. Our main task
in this chapter is to find a way to reduce these 52 variables
into one or more scales representing the status of women
relative to men, or selected aspects of that broad concept.
Even if there were no valid theoretical reason for this reduction process, the sheer number of variables would force it
upon us. (To examine the relationships between 46 independent variables and 12 control variables on the one hand
and our 52 dependent variables would require inspection of
3,016 bivariate statistical relationships!) Yet we have a theoretical reason for this reduction as well, one stated most
clearly over half a century ago by Robert Lowie (1920, p.
187): "First of all, it should be noted that the treatment of
woman is one thing, her legal status another, her opportunities for public activity still another, while the character and
extent of her labors belong again to a distinct category. Whatever correlations exist between any two of these aspects are
empirical; conceptually they are diverse, and only confusion
can result from ignoring the fact."

Lowie's statement calls into question the existence of any
such general phenomenon as "the status of women," but he
also notes that there may be correlations between separate
aspects of this vague concept. In this chapter we will examine
just what the empirical interrelationships are among different
aspects of what we have supposed to be this general concept
of the status of women. Can many of these items be grouped
into one coherent scale measuring our general conception?

95

Or do various aspects of the status of women vary quite independently in our sample, so that knowing, for example, that women hold political offices in a particular culture will not allow us to predict anything about their economic rights or their role in religious affairs? In this chapter we will seek to answer these questions, and in the process to construct the scale or scales of the status of women that we will use to test our hypotheses in the following chapter.

When we start examining the pattern of associations among our 52 dependent variables, it turns out that most are rather weak. We will not burden the reader here with the entire matrix of intercorrelations.[1] Instead we present selected items in table 1.

TABLE 1
INTERCORRELATIONS AMONG SELECTED DEPENDENT VARIABLES

	DV 7	DV 10	DV 15	DV 35	DV 50
DV 1: Sex of gods and spirits	−.03	−.02	−.10	.26	.09
DV 7: Sex of local political leaders	—	.10	.16	−.15	.03
DV 10: Relative contribution of women to subsistence		—	−.00	−.11	.23
DV 15: Relative inheritance rights			—	−.06	.17
DV 35: Relative ease of divorce				—	.26
DV 50: Machismo concerns					—

NOTE: Ns vary from 50 to the full 93 cultures.

1. Before correlations were computed all of the final "ambiguous, no information" categories in the dependent variables were recoded as blanks, thus removing them from the calculations. Otherwise our calculations simply used the numbers assigned to the categories in chapter IV. Since our scales are ordinal rather than interval (i.e., the categories are ordered, but the particular numbers assigned are ar-

Clearly the correlations in this table are not strong, even when compared with previous cross-cultural research. In general a correlation of about .2 would be expected to occur only five times out of one hundred by chance alone in a sample of this size under assumptions of randomness. In the small matrix above there are three correlations above this figure, but also many near zero figures and negative signs. The full matrix reveals more or less the same pattern. We examined the latter matrix using a statistical searching procedure called cluster analysis,[2] which locates clusters of variables that vary together in a sample. If there were a general phenomenon we could call the status of women in our pool of 52 dependent variables, we could expect to start with a single large cluster with many variables in it. Instead we found many clusters, none of which included more than five variables.

The next step was to examine the clusters to see if they made sense. By looking at clusters and examining the correlations of other variables with those making up each cluster, we formed our final dependent variable scales. We used

---

bitrary, with no guarantee that the difference between a score of 4 and 3 is as important as that between a score of 3 and 2), we should properly be examining matrices of ordinal measures of association, such as gamma or tau, rather than the product moment correlation statistic r. However, the computer programs available made it much more laborious and costly to calculate ordinal association statistics for 52 by 52 matrix, and since we are simply sorting for clusters of variables rather than testing hypotheses, we felt we were on safe grounds using r.

2. For a general description of this procedure see Wallace (1968), p. 522. Essentially the procedure searches for the highest intercorrelation in the entire matrix. It then searches the rest of the matrix for any other variables that have a correlation above a certain minimum size (we chose a value of $r = .2$) with the first two variables found. All variables that meet this minimum criterion constitute a *cluster*. They are removed from further calculations, and then the computer begins the procedure again by searching the remainder of the matrix for the highest correlation left. It keeps taking clusters from the matrix until no more can be initiated.

three criteria: that at least three items had to constitute each scale, that the average inter-item correlation among the variables in each scale had to exceed $r = .2$, and that the items had to have some sort of interpretable common meaning. We found nine of such scales,[3] representing what seem to be distinct aspects of the status of women relative to men. Thus instead of a single global scale of women's status, we have scales for nine separate parts of our core concept. The fact that no coherent unitary scale could be constructed is a fact of considerable importance to which we shall return later.

The nine final scales, and their composite items, are as follows:

DVS 1: Property control scale (Abbreviated: Property control)
 DV 15: Inheritance rights
 DV 16: Dwelling ownership
 DV 17: Control of fruits of male labor
 DV 18: Control of fruits of joint labor
 DV 19: Control of fruits of female labor
Average inter-item correlation = .28 (A 4-point scale.)
High score = more control by women

DVS 2: Power of women in kinship contexts (Abbreviated: Kin power)
 DV 8: Kin-group political leadership
 DV 31: Preferred marriage forms
 DV 32: Multiple spouses
 DV 33: Levirate absence
Average inter-item correlation = .413 (A 3-point scale.)
High score = less kin-group domination of women

3. The reader will note, then, that cluster analysis has been used as a time-saving convenience in searching a large matrix of intercorrelations, rather than as the final arbiter of scale composition. Each scale was constructed by giving equal weight to each item. In cases of missing data the scale score is an average of the scores of each of the items for which data were present.

DVS 3:   Value placed on the lives of women (Abbreviated: Value of life)
   DV 41:   Child preference
   DV 42:   Infanticide
   DV 45:   Beating of spouse
Average inter-item correlation = .267 (A 3-point scale.)
High score = less bias against women

DVS 4:   Value placed on the labor of women (Abbreviated: Value of labor)
   DV 10:   Relative contribution of women to subsistence
   DV 11:   Relative subsistence effort
   DV 30:   Marriage finance (with direction reversed)
Average inter-item correlation = .280 (A 5-point scale.)
High score = greater value of women's labor

DVS 5:   Domestic authority
   DV 38:   Final authority over infants
   DV 39:   Final authority over children
   DV 46:   Lack of male dominance over wives
Average inter-item correlation = .375 (A 4-point scale.)
High score = more domestic authority of women

DVS 6:   Ritualized separation of the sexes (Abbreviated: Ritualized female solidarity)
   DV 12:   Exclusively male work organizations
   DV 13:   Exclusively female work organizations
   DV 24:   Menstrual taboo scale
   DV 48:   Female initiation ceremonies
   DV 51:   Lack of a belief in general female inferiority
Average inter-item correlation = .247 (A 3-point scale.)
High score = greater ritualized separation of the sexes

DVS 7:   Control over women's marital and sexual lives (Abbreviated: Control of sex)
   DV 21:   Lack of a premarital double standard
   DV 22:   Lack of an extramarital double standard

DV 36:   Remarriage ease
DV 37:   Relative ages at first marriage
Average inter-item correlation = .242 (A 3-point scale.)
High score = less bias in favor of men

DVS 8:   Ritualized fear of women (Abbreviated: Ritu-
          alized fear)
DV 6:   Funeral ceremony elaborateness
DV 27:   Absence of danger of sexual activity
DV 50:   Lack of machismo concerns
Average inter-item correlation = .247 (A 3-point scale.)
High score = less ritualized fear of women

DVS 9:   Male-female joint participation (Abbreviated:
          Joint participation)
DV 9:   Participation in warfare
DV 14:   Absence of work segregation
DV 47:   Participation in community meetings and
          activities
Average inter-item correlation = .229 (A 3-point scale.)
High score = more joint participation

The reader will note that inevitably these scales are influenced by the items in our pool, in particular the number of separate variables with meanings that are similar. However, this is not the entire story, since many of these scales contain items that are not obviously similar, and other items that might be assumed to fit with others do not. (For example, wife to husband deference—DV 40—does not scale with domestic authority; women's ability to have extramarital affairs— DV 23—does not scale with control over women's sex lives.)

In DVS 4 the finding that our scale of marriage finance correlates with the proportional contribution of women to subsistence accords with that of Heath (1958; see also Boserup, 1970, p. 48). Substantial bride prices tend to be customary in societies where women contribute much to subsistence. Such payments should not be thought of as indicating the "sale" of females, but as a recognition of the loss

100

of the woman's work services by her family and a corresponding gain by her husband's family.

Our scale DVS 6, which we refer to as indicating ritualized separation of the sexes, is composed predominantly of items that Young and Bacdayan (1965) say are measures of "social rigidity." This concept refers to a relative lack of intercommunication among parts of a social system—produced in this case by the sharp separation of men and women. However, Young and Bacdayan argue that "social rigidity" (which they admittedly measure somewhat differently) is associated with low status for women. We find no such pattern—in fact our scale includes a measure of the *absence* of any belief in female inferiority (DV 51). Thus our scale for ritualized separation of the sexes does not indicate the subjugation of women and may tap something that is favorable for women—their ability to unite together with other women in the community at large for important activities. For this reason we leave this scale in a form in which a high score indicates greater ritualized separation of the sexes, rather than reversing it. We refer to this scale in abbreviated form as "ritualized female solidarity" to stress this positive meaning, even though we recognize that a part of the scale indicates that males also achieve some group solidarity.[4] (Note

4. Our findings here also differ from those in a recent cross-cultural study by Zelman (1974). She interprets female pollution rituals, including menstrual taboos, as ways in which cultures symbolically make sharp distinctions between the roles of men and women, distinctions that are in turn associated with low power of, and respect for, women. Women in Zelman's study have greater power and esteem when these rituals are absent, and where there is much interchange and sharing of roles between the sexes. We have not systematically coded for female pollution rituals in general, but our menstrual taboo scale is *positively* associated with women's collective work organizations and with the absence of any belief in the general inferiority of women. Our finding, in contrast to Zelman's, suggests that in the relations between the sexes, separate is not necessarily unequal (to the disadvantage of women). In fact ritual emphasis on the differences between men's and women's roles may give women collective solidarity that they lack when a culture emphasizes the sharing of roles

also that our menstrual taboo scale—DV 24—also enters this scale as a *positive* item with stricter taboos associated with the *lack* of a belief in female inferiority.)

We also note, since we were originally unsure about the relevance to status of our item dealing with the relative ages of men and women at marriage, that we find that this variable scales with items concerned with control over women's marital and sexual lives, with "women are older than men at marriage" associated with other items indicating more stringent controls on the sex lives of women. Conversely, a large positive gap between men's and women's marriage ages is associated with more equal sexual restrictions on males and females. It is not immediately obvious why this should be, although one can speculate at least that where men marry much younger women it doesn't make much sense to have strong restrictions on women remarrying since, given the generally longer life spans of women, such a society will produce many widows.

The meaning of DVS 8 is perhaps not so clear as the other scales, but the items seem to have some relationship to the sort of men's ritualized insecurity or fear of women that is sometimes said to lead to exaggerated displays of male superiority. (This, we recall, was the argument underlying the sexual envy hypothesis in chapter III.) It is also not entirely clear why DVS 9, dealing with joint participation of men and women, should end up as a separate scale from DVS 6, which seems to be dealing with the opposite. From examining the items we can see that those in DVS 6 refer more to ritualized separation, whereas those in DVS 9 refer to less ritualized forms of joint or separate activities. Yet we will still need to examine how these two scales relate to each other and to our other variables.

---

between husband and wife. Given these contrasting results, obtained with different concepts, procedures, and samples, clearly more research is needed on the relationships among pollution rituals, sex-role differences, collective organization of women, and aspects of sexual equality and inequality.

Now that we have formed our scales, we find that only 33 out of our original 52 dependent variables are included. The remaining 19 items could not be formed into any scales meeting our established criteria (interpretable scales with at least three items, and with average inter-item correlations in excess of .2). The items left out are:

DV 1:   Sex of gods and spirits
DV 2:   Sex of mythical founders
DV 3:   Sex of shamans
DV 4:   Sex of witches
DV 5:   Religious ceremony participation
DV 7:   Local political leaders
DV 20:   Domestic work
DV 23:   Women's extramarital affairs
DV 25:   Roles in procreation
DV 26:   Strength of sex drives
DV 28:   Elders arrange marriages
DV 29:   Couple's marital say
DV 34:   Moves at marriage
DV 35:   Divorce rights
DV 40:   Deference scale
DV 43:   Training for adult duties
DV 44:   Relative punishment
DV 49:   Belief in change in women's status
DV 52:   Women's informal influence

One pattern to note is that the failure to form scales was greatest for items in the religious realm. Only one out of seven items in that section (that dealing with the elaborateness of funerals) ended up in our scales. This indicates that the independent variation of religious and magical practices and beliefs cross-culturally is greater than in the other social realms. Since none of the variables listed above could be formed into acceptable scales,[5] with one exception they will

5. We should report that two scales did emerge that met our statistical criteria, but which we found uninterpretable. We list them

not be used further in our analysis of the status of women. This exception is the final item, DV 52. For reasons already stated, we have a particular interest in finding out how the informal influence of women varies cross-culturally and how this variable relates to aspects of their formal status. For this reason we decided to retain this one single variable (for which high score equals presence of greater informal influence of women) along with our nine dependent variable scales, and all will be used together in testing our hypotheses in the next chapter.

We should also acknowledge that these scales, the result of empirical search procedures, fail to fit any obvious analytical scheme. We did not find separate scales for the religious, political, economic, sexual, and domestic status of women; neither did we find scales of women's treatment, their legal rights, their opportunities for public activity, and the character and extent of their labors, as Lowie suggested. Instead we get a number of scales covering different aspects of social life and of the role of women relative to men, and we are not aware of simplifications that will allow us to fit these several scales into a smaller number of conceptual boxes. Therefore we will simply have to see how each of these scales relates to our hypotheses.

We can, however, examine the pattern of associations of the scales with each other. Although our empirical search procedure tends to group items into scales in such a way that correlations of particular items with other scales are not high, it is not clear what types of associations we should expect to find among our ten separate scales. We have not used a search procedure that would have guaranteed statistical in-

---

here, and invite the reader to examine them and consider whether they are anything more than empirical flukes: cluster 1—DV 3, sex of shamans, DV 28, elders arranging marriages, and DV 34, moves at marriage; cluster 2—DV 2, mythical founders, DV 20, domestic work, and DV 29, couple's marital say.

dependence among the scales.[6] Thus we cannot tell whether to expect independence or perhaps some pattern of significant associations among these ten variables. Here we show the actual matrix of intercorrelations among our nine dependent variable scales and DV 52.

The relationships in table 2 are generally weak, and in some cases they are in a direction opposite to our initial expectations. The only clear cluster that emerges in this matrix is the group of positive relationships among our scales for the value of women's lives (DVS 3), the domestic authority of women (DVS 5), and ritualized separation of the sexes (DVS 6). Should we simplify our task by combining these three into a single, more general, scale? By examining table 2 we can see that the associations among these three scales are modest in strength, and that each scale has a somewhat different pattern of associations with the other seven scales. Therefore we decided to retain all ten scales in the subsequent analysis, while keeping in mind the associations these particular three scales have.

We also note here that our measure of joint social participation has a relationship essentially of zero with our scale of ritualized separation of the sexes. This indicates that these are not simply two different measures of the separate or joint activities of men and women. The association of our ritualized female solidarity scale with two scales dealing with the domestic status of women but not with our scale of joint participation does not accord with the conclusion reached by Sacks (1971, p. 5), based on a comparison of four African cultures, that collective organization of the labor of women

6. Previous cross-cultural research has relied heavily on factor analysis with orthogonal rotations, which produces such statistically independent scales. See, for example, Gouldner and Peterson, 1962. However, since our variables and the variables in most cross-cultural research cannot meet the strict statistical requirements of the factor analysis procedure, we have chosen not to use the technique in this study. For a general description of factor analysis and its applications see Rummel, 1970.

TABLE 2
CORRELATIONS AMONG DEPENDENT VARIABLE SCALES

	DVS 2	DVS 3	DVS 4	DVS 5	DVS 6	DVS 7	DVS 8	DVS 9	DV 52
DVS 1: Property control	.01	.06	−.03	.21*	.05	−.14	.18	−.04	.01
DVS 2: Kin power	—	−.11	.05	.00	−.28*	−.09	−.03	−.13	−.10
DVS 3: Value of life		—	.09	.22*	.25*	.03	.04	−.03	.08
DVS 4: Value of labor			—	.15	−.09	.07	.14	−.03	.02
DVS 5: Domestic authority				—	.27*	.07	.16	−.11	−.00
DVS 6: Ritualized female solidarity					—	.22*	.09	.00	.02
DVS 7: Control of sex						—	.03	−.25	−.09
DVS 8: Ritualized fear							—	.05	.03
DVS 9: Joint participation								—	−.00
DV 52: Informal influence									—

NOTE: Ns are all in the range 88-93.

* = relationship likely to occur on basis of chance alone less than five times out of one hundred ($p \leqq .05$).

(part of our ritualized female solidarity scale) is a crucial determinant of the ability of women to enter into egalitarian relationships *beyond* the household. The influence of this "separate but equal" solidarity of women seems to be more limited.

The rest of table 2 shows a pattern of little or no association among the variables. Clearly the value of women's labor (DVS 4), ritualized fear of women (DVS 8) and informal influence (DV 52) scales are virtually independent of any of the other scales, with low correlations and with negative signs almost as often as positive ones. The property control scale (DVS 1) also has a pattern of low and often negative associations with the other variables, although here there is one stronger relationship between women owning property and women having substantial power within the home (DVS 5). Other relationships in the table do not seem worth mentioning. We can conclude by saying that, except for the three scales noted (DVS 3, 5, and 6) our matrix in table 2 lacks a consistent pattern of statistical associations among our separate measures of the status of women. In addition to the generally low levels of the correlation coefficients, we note that instead of a generally positive pattern of associations among our measures of the status of women, about 40% of the signs are negative. We must conclude that cross-culturally we are dealing with variables that are virtually independent, again with the exception of the three scales mentioned.

Our conclusion, then, is that Lowie was basically correct in his cautionary statement. While small groups of discrete measures of aspects of the status of women can be formed into coherent scales, and while a few of these have consistent patterns of association with some others, the thrust of our results is that there is a large amount of independent variation in aspects of what we have been considering the general status of women.[7] We did not make specific pre-

7. Another recent study voices a similar sentiment: "Roles may be differentiated by sex within each of the major institutional aspects of

dictions about what pattern we would find, but the degree of independent variation (or lack of association) is quite striking. We find that knowing how much of the subsistence in a particular culture is produced by women will not help us to predict what sort of property rights women will have, or whether they will have their sexual and marital lives severely restricted. Likewise, the fact that men monopolize the property in a particular culture does not allow us to predict how women's lives will be valued or how much informal influence women will have in that culture. Clearly we are dealing with very complex phenomena.

Let us drive this point home by taking a brief look at the relative position of women in two of the cultures that form part of our sample. Our first example is the Twana (culture 133 in the Murdock and White standard sample). We rely here mainly on a description of the Twana circa 1860, as reconstructed by W. W. Elmendorf (1960) on the basis of the accounts of native informants (see also Elmendorf, 1948; Eells, 1877). The Twana were a group of about one thousand Indians who were located in the Hood Canal region of western Washington. Their economy was based on a highly productive combination of fishing, hunting, and gathering, with salmon fishing by far the most important contributor to their diet. Descent was traced bilaterally, and upon marriage the bride came to live with the groom's family. The Twana were seminomadic, concentrating in permanent settlements of many families during the winter months, and dispersing in groups of one or a few families for the summer to fish, hunt, and gather food. They did not engage in warfare with other communities, but were tied to them by networks of elaborate and ritualized exchanges of food and other goods usually

---

the social system: the family, the economy, the political system, the religious system, etc., and the patterns in one aspect may not be consistent with those of another. To give an example in terms of sex status, it is not difficult to imagine a society in which women play an important part in family decision-making but are discriminated against in the occupational sphere" (quoted from Levine, 1966, p. 186).

referred to in the ethnographic literature by the term *pot-latches*. There were no formal political offices, but generally the male head of the wealthiest family in the community was considered the community leader and spokesman. The Twana were divided into wealthy and poor families, depending upon their accumulated property and their ability to host potlatch exchanges, but the boundary between the two groups was not rigidly fixed. The Twana also owned slaves, apparently obtained from other tribes who took them as war captives. These slaves were considered private property and could be exchanged, and intermarriage of Twana with them was strictly forbidden. The Twana were able to acquire from nature most of what they needed to live, and they engaged in only small-scale barter exchange with other tribes during the period before intensive acculturation by the whites (potlatch exchanges were mainly aimed at competing for prestige, rather than at acquiring unavailable items).

There were a number of clear kinds of sexual inequality among the Twana. For one thing men contributed much more to subsistence than women. Men did most of the fishing and all of the hunting, while women gathered the mollusks, roots, and berries that formed secondary items in the Twana diet. Women were forbidden to have contact with some canoes and weapons used by men in fishing and hunting. They could troll in the salt water for fish, but this was of minor importance compared to the river net fishing engaged in by men. Sometimes men also engaged in root digging. On balance men provided the bulk of the food. Both men and women were expected to be generous in distributing the fruits of their labors to others, but men generally had much more to distribute. Men seem to have been the hosts for the large potlatch feasts, to which other communities and even other tribes were invited. Men built and owned the houses, the informal community leaders were all men, and the few full-time specialists in the community (canoe makers, sea mammal hunters) were also men. The one exception to the latter pattern is that a few women became shamans, although

109

mostly this was a role taken by men. Only men could take extra spouses, although only the wealthiest men were polygynous. A clear double standard existed in both premarital and extramarital sex. Young boys were encouraged to seduce women, while young women were strictly supervised and discouraged from responding, particularly among the wealthier families. In cases of adultery the woman was viewed as at fault, and she might be divorced or even killed, while the husband's infidelity was viewed as fairly harmless. We see a number of patterns here that seem to suggest general male domination of women.

Yet in other areas of social life the Twana give quite a different impression. A woman could acquire property, including slaves, from her father or her mother. This property was not taken over by the husband, and a woman could independently pass property on to her own children. Relations between spouses seem to have been fairly harmonious. Men did not demand subordination or emphasize sexual conquests, parents played a fairly equal role in raising and disciplining children, and the wife was not required to make extreme displays of deference toward her husband. There is no evidence that wife beating was frequent or approved, or that there was a preference for male children or female infanticide. Both bride and groom were fairly young at marriage, and each had an equal voice in marriage decisions (which were freer among the poor families than among the wealthy). Divorce and remarriage were also relatively equally available to women and men among the poorer Twana, although among the wealthy a woman could not initiate a divorce as easily as a man could. There was some fear of contamination from women, primarily from menstrual blood, but there was also a belief in pollution from contact with semen in sexual intercourse. Women worked in cooperative work groups with other women, they observed strict menstrual taboos and had their solidarity reinforced further by elaborate female initiation rituals. Men sometimes hunted or fished together in groups, but they lacked any comparable male

110

initiation ritual or secret society. In fact the Twana had secret societies and sweat houses that both men and women belonged to and used. Women also participated actively in all community gatherings and feasts and may even have hosted some of the latter (e.g., at the end of a daughter's initiation). The religious life of the Twana centered on the quest of individuals for guardian spirits, whose powers were felt necessary for almost all human activities. There were a few guardian spirits associated with male or female tasks, but most could be sought by either sex. Women could even acquire guardian spirits known for giving hunting prowess, although women would gain other qualities from these spirits. Occasionally a young man could even be directed on a vision quest by an experienced older female relative rather than by a male, given the equal knowledge women had acquired in this area. Finally, among the Twana, women did most of the domestic work, but men helped out in some ways—by doing some of the cooking and by dressing skins and trimming fur for clothing.

We have not covered all of our equality-inequality themes in this brief discussion, but we see that the Twana had important areas of rough equality—in domestic authority, in the value placed on women's lives, in joint participation with men, in ritualized female solidarity, and in the most important spheres of religious life. These areas of rough equality qualify our initial impression of male dominance, and if our sources are any guide the Twana did not feel there was anything inconsistent about these patterns. For example, men's dominance in subsistence work did not lead the Twana to feel that women were not qualified to seek guardian spirits, and women's skills in the latter area did not lead them to feel they should have a larger role in hunting and fishing.

For purposes of comparison, let us now examine a culture from a very different part of the world, the Garo (culture 69 in the Murdock and White sample). The Garo are one of the hill tribes of northern India, described as of 1955 by Robbins Burling (1963; see also Choudhury, 1958; Ehrenfels, 1947;

and Nakane, 1967). The Garo lived in a hilly region in the state of Assam where they practiced slash and burn agriculture as their main form of subsistence. Dry field rice was the major crop, supplemented by millet, corn, taro, manioc, cotton, and a variety of other crops. The villagers raised pigs, chickens, and other small domestic animals, and there was a minor amount of fishing and hunting done also. The Garo had been in contact with the people of the nearby plains for hundreds of years, and before the British established their rule in the area they were already trading in the money economy of the markets run by people of the plains in order to supplement the output of their own fields. The village studied by Burling had maintained its traditional economic, kinship, and religious system fairly intact in spite of these contacts—for example, the villagers had not converted to either Christianity or Hinduism, the major classical religions of the area. The Garo lived in permanent villages surrounded by their agricultural fields. Portions of these fields were cleared, burned, and cultivated for a two-year period, after which they were allowed to lie unused for another 6-8 years while other portions were cultivated. The Garo practiced matrilineal descent, and generally males came in from other kin groups and villages to marry and live with their brides. There were no formal classes, and the shifting agriculture and ready availability of land kept inequality in check. Nevertheless, some families managed their farming and trading better than others and were able to build better houses, buy valuable heirloom items, and give large feasts for other families during village festivals. There were no slaves, and intercommunity warfare and headhunting had been suppressed by the British after the 1860s. Each village had one or more headmen, but their duties were mainly ceremonial, and they had no real political power. Beyond the village there was a post of judge or arbitrator for disputes in the entire region, a post to which a Garo was appointed by the Indian government (formerly by the British). Outside of these offices there was no formal political leadership, and

112

many issues were settled by informal discussion and financial compensation between two contending matrilineal kin groups.

At first glance there are a number of features of Garo life that suggest extensive sexual equality, or even some advantages for women. The farming work was shared fairly equally by men and women, although some individual tasks were sex-typed. Neither a man nor a woman could get along easily without a partner of the opposite sex to help in farming. Women did most of the domestic work, but men helped some with child care and with cooking for ceremonial meals, and they made all of the baskets. Community gatherings and celebrations involved both men and women, although they often danced and sat separately. Houses were built by men, but the inheritance of housing and other valuables went formally to the daughter, although the daughter's husband gained considerable control over the management of family property. Divorce was discouraged, but if it did occur either sex might initiate it, and the male generally left the family property intact when he left, taking only his personal clothing and effects. Restrictions on, and punishment of, extramarital sex were fairly equal, although for premarital sex the girl was in more danger of stigmatization, especially if she became pregnant, than was the boy. The relationships between spouses seemed fairly equal, with no extreme deference customs, no condoning of wife beating, and no special concern with male domination and sexual conquest. The ideal was one of equal cooperation and substantial sharing between husband and wife. There was a preference for girl children as potential heirs, but no evidence of male infanticide, and young boys and girls were raised and treated fairly similarly.

Perhaps the most distinctive feature of Garo life in terms of sexual equality was the system of marriage choice, in which the female's side (and often the female herself) had more say than the male's. A boy might flirt with unmarried girls, but he was not given any culturally approved ways of suggesting marriage. If a girl was not chosen as heir to her family's house and property she was expected to take the

113

initiative in finding a husband, going to the market and participating in local festivals and other activities while looking over the field. If she settled on a particular boy she indicated her choice to her father. If the girl had been chosen as the heir she might have less say, and her father would look over the prospects, perhaps consulting with the mother of a boy in the appropriate kin group (preferably the matrilineage to which he belonged, so that he would be the uncle of his daughter's spouse). In either case the actual marriage was brought about by "groom capture." Several young males from the girl's lineage were sent out to catch the unsuspecting groom-to-be and drag him back, kicking and yelling, to the girl's village for the wedding. The boy could veto the marriage by running away repeatedly and refusing to stay with the girl, but still the initiative rested with the girl's family, and often with the girl herself. This custom provides a clear contrast with the image some writers have had of "primitive" marriage as based originally on the forcible abduction and rape of women, although it must be noted that among the Garo the actual abductors (and, in the case of a girl picked as heir, the main initiator) were not women but other men.

When we look at other areas of Garo social life, we begin to see more evidence of sexual inequality. Only men might have extra spouses, and a widow had somewhat more difficulty in remarrying than a widower, since her new spouse had to be promised a second, previously unmarried woman as well. Every man was seen as entitled to at least one "new" wife, but some women ended up married to husbands who were not new—i.e., to widowers and divorcés—and these women were not similarly entitled to a second husband. The main disciplinarians of older children were males—the matrilineal uncles who continued to reside in the village to supervise their sisters' children—although the parents shared this burden from day to day. Young boys left their parents' home at about the age of 12 to live in the village bachelor house until marriage. There they had relative freedom from parental and avuncular supervision, but their special status

114

was not ritualized by any sort of initiation ceremony. Girls did not leave home in this manner and were more closely supervised. The solidarity of women was reflected in the system of matrilineal descent, but it was not emphasized or ritualized by female initiation, menstrual taboos, or by large-scale women's work groups. In most community activities women formed a unit with their husbands, rather than with large numbers of other women. Religious ceremonies were largely in the hands of the men. The men made the altars on which sacrifices to the gods were offered, they slaughtered the animals involved, and they provided the ritual specialists who officiated. In communitywide sacrifices the organizer was often the village headman, who had little formal power outside of his central role in festival religious observances. (The appointed judge or arbitrator for the region was also a male.) The headman was generally the husband of the oldest woman in the senior household of the village, and this man passed the post on to his son-in-law. Other men also used the periodic village festivals to organize and host feasts for other families that, like the Twana potlatches, served to increase their prestige (although these feasts might affect the prestige of the entire household, and not just that of the hosts).

Garo agricultural land was periodically rotated, as described earlier. All families in the village had the right to farm a part of those fields that were opened up for new cultivation in any year, and the plots within these fields were not considered privately owned, although often a family received roughly the same area they tilled in the previous farming cycle. However, the Garo did recognize the private ownership of titles to village land. These titles did not give their owners the right to till that land, since those rights were governed by the rotation system. Nevertheless, these titles were considered valuable, they could be bought and sold, and disputes over their possession and inheritance could lead to suits and outside arbitration. These land titles were owned not by women, but by individual men—generally by the vil-

115

lage headman and a few of the other wealthy men in the community. Men also owned the most important devices used to store wealth—the metal gongs that were used in village festivals, and which could also be bought and sold. Men also did all of the important marketing among the Garo. They made the major sales of cotton and other cash crops, and purchased major food, clothing, and other items. Women did some smaller trading (e.g., selling rice beer to passersby), and they could keep their earnings to spend on either individual or family needs. Yet it is clear that in both feasting and marketing men had more control over the family economy than either their restricted inheritance rights or their equal subsistence role would lead one to expect. In reviewing the total picture of Garo life we can see that two sets of males—the brothers and the husbands of Garo women —had important powers and advantages that qualify our initial impression of sexual equality.

If these two examples have served their purpose, the reader should see the inappropriateness of asking in which culture *the* status of women is higher. We can compare the domestic authority of women relative to men in the two cultures, or their subsistence contribution or property rights, but the total picture is of a series of pluses and minuses that are different in each culture and that cannot be summed up easily to form an overall measure of women's status. These very brief descriptions of two cultures illustrate concretely the complexity that is characteristic of most of our other cultures, a complexity that our statistical manipulations portray more comprehensively, but perhaps less vividly.

Our findings lead us to conclude that we can find no evidence for the existence of any general "status of women" complex that varies consistently from culture to culture. Rather, with tenuous exceptions, aspects of what we have called the status of women tend to vary independently from culture to culture. We should pause to reflect on this finding, since in much of current discourse the existence of such a complex is simply assumed. People often argue about

116

whether women have higher status in society X or in society Y; or about what kinds of social change will produce the greatest improvement in the status of women; or about which of two variables is the better indicator of the status of women in a society. All of these modes of thinking, modes that have guided our study up to this point, are based upon an initial and very basic assumption that there is such a thing as the general status of women. Now we find out it isn't so! The intuitive logic of the idea of the general status of women is not borne out by the empirical reality of 93 cultures. It seems that it no longer makes sense to say that women have higher status in society X than in society Y, but only that a certain restricted type of female rights or privileges is scored higher in society X, while perhaps another type is higher in society Y. Moreover, we cannot say which of two variables is a better indicator of the status of women because we now are led to doubt the existence of such a general phenomenon.[8] Once this uncomfortably complicating fact is accepted we can at least gain some understanding of why debates about "the status of women" have generated so much heat and so little light in recent years. In much of both the scholarly and popular literature the existence of a general syndrome of women's status is taken for granted, and it is assumed that its various aspects tend to be highly related to each other. Yet this turns out not to be the case cross-culturally. To expand on a familiar analogy, a comparison of different indicators of this assumed general concept turns out to be a case of trying to compare apples, oranges, bananas, kumquats, and so forth.

Once we acknowledge the complexity of the phenomena, another set of difficult questions arise. If we cannot locate a

8. To be precise we are not saying that no *conception* such as the general status of women can exist. Clearly people can formulate whatever theoretical constructs they wish to. What we are saying is that such a conception will not be useful since, whatever indicators are chosen to measure it, they will be found to have weak or negligible associations cross-culturally. Since a systematic pattern of correlations is lacking, empirically this conception is not useful.

117

general status of women concept empirically, is there any sense in continuing to talk about *the* status of women? If instead of a general status variable we get many separate variables, is there any reason to think that these separate variables have any status implications for women at all? Is our use of this term "the status of women" perhaps just a reflection of our urge to impose Western concepts of status and power on societies and cultures having very different conceptions? In answering these questions our numbers and tables are of little help. If we had found large numbers of our dependent variables associated in a consistent way, this cross-cultural regularity would have assuaged our doubts. Since that was not our result, we must turn again to our dependent variable scales to consider, on simply logical grounds, whether the meaning of sexual inequality we have imputed to them is intrinsic, or simply an arbitrary and misleading label.

Our first dependent variable scale, dealing with property control, seems to have intrinsic power or status implications. While cultures may differ in the importance they attribute to property ownership, wherever property rights exist, more property seems to be thought of as better than less property (even when the accumulation of property is carried out partly in order to be subsequently distributed to others), and when men have more property rights than women it is hard to see how this could fail to have some status implications. To the author the status implications are also fairly clear with our scales for the power of women in kinship contexts (DVS 2—although here the levirate item is not so obvious), for our scale of the value placed on women's lives (DVS 3), for domestic authority (DVS 5), the control over women's marital and sexual lives (DVS 7—although here age at first marriage is not so clear), and the ritualized fear of women (DVS 8—although here the danger of sexual activity to men might not imply the inferiority of women). However, the other scales do not have such clear status connotations. The contribution of women to subsistence (in DVS 4) could, as we mentioned in chapter III, be seen either as an indication

118

of the value of women to society or as an indication of their subordination to less diligent men. Ritualized separation of the sexes (DVS 6) was first thought to have negative status implications, although empirically we discovered it had modest positive associations with certain aspects of the domestic position of women. With our scale for male-female joint participation (DVS 9) it is not clear that either segregation in work or lack of female participation in warfare implies negative status for women, although exclusion of women from community gatherings and activities does have more of a negative "sense" to it. Finally, it is not clear whether our measure of the informal influence of women (DV 52) would be viewed positively or negatively. Perhaps where women have much informal influence it is a measure of their lack of formal influence, and this forces them to work "behind the scenes" to get their way. (See here the comments of Lowie, 1920, pp. 188-189.)

In sum, we cannot be certain that all of our scales have the meanings we originally presumed for them. Some of our ten scales seem to be measuring aspects of the role of women or their relationship to men that, on reflection, cannot be said to have clear status implications. This does not mean that these scales are not of interest to us. It does mean that we can no longer use the shorthand of talking about "the status of women," but must adopt the more cumbersome but accurate practice of referring to our ten scales as measures of different aspects of the relative status, roles, and relationship of the sexes.

Every culture has some conception of the position of men and women in social life, and the particular combination of traits that makes up such conceptions varies a great deal from society to society. Our data do not lead us to conclude that there is no common ground across societies in discrete aspects of the relationship between the sexes. However, they do indicate that there is little or no necessary connection cross-culturally among these separate aspects of the relative status, roles, and relationship of the sexes. What to a West-

119

ern mind may seem to be contradictory combinations of high and low positions of women in different areas of social life occur commonly in our sample, and in fact they are the general rule. In the next chapter we investigate what other cultural traits are associated with particular high or low values on our individual scales. By doing this we may explain some part of the cross-cultural variation of these selected aspects of the position of men and women. However, we cannot now hope to explain how and why the status of women varies cross-culturally. The complexities of social life in 93 cultures have not yielded to the simplifications of the researcher's conceptual categories or to the computer's manipulations.

CHAPTER VI

Why the Status of Women Varies

WE have now settled upon ten separate measures we regard as aspects of the status, the roles, and the relationship of women relative to men. Our final major question concerns why these measures vary cross-culturally. In this chapter we will be testing each of the hypotheses presented in chapter III by looking at the statistical relationships between the independent variables involved and our ten scales in our effort to answer this "why" question. We will search for the important cultural and social structural features that are associated with high and low ratings on these dependent variable scales. In our analysis we constructed contingency tables representing all of the hypothesized relationships. Because the number of associations we are examining is still quite large (the associations of 46 independent variables and 12 control variables with 10 dependent variable scales, or 580 relationships in all), it is not practicable to present the tables here. Rather, we will use the summary ordinal measure of association gamma (Goodman and Kruskal, 1954) to judge the results. We also report the significance level achieved by the chi-square statistic for the same tables if it surpasses the .05 probability level.[1]

1. Gamma is the probability that any two cases drawn at random from a contingency table will have the same ordering on the two variables involved minus the probability that such a pair will have a different ordering. The result varies between -1 and $+1$, with larger values indicating a stronger relationship. Values of gamma cannot be compared directly with the correlation statistic r used in the previous chapter. We can illustrate the sorts of relationships that yield gammas of different sizes here, using associations that will appear in table 3. There we will see that the association between cultures using plow technology and our property control scale is gamma $= -.22$,

Since we will be viewing and discussing a large number of these summary tables, several guides for the reader are needed. Our ten measures of the position of women are at the left of each table. A high score for each scale has the same meaning as indicated in chapter V, although now we are not confident that in each case a high score means high

---

while the association of the plow with our domestic authority scale is stronger, with gamma = −.55. The crosstabulations that yielded these statistics are as follows:

Property control scale scores:	*Plow* Absent	*Plow* Present	Domestic authority scale scores:	*Plow* Absent	*Plow* Present
1	5%	4%	1	6%	17%
2	15	32	2	19	35
3	70	52	3	35	39
4	10	12	4	40	9
Total	100%	100%	Total	100%	100%
N	67	25	N	65	23

In both tables there is a negative relationship, with higher scale scores where the plow is absent. Yet the table on the left reveals a weaker relationship than the one on the right, attributable primarily to plow technology affecting the number of cultures with scores two versus three. The negative association is visible in all rows of the table on the right, and this explains the larger gamma value for that table. There may be some question about the appropriateness of using significance tests in the first place, and there is a long and contentious literature in sociology over when to use and not to use them. Essentially surpassing the .05 significance level means a statistical association of a size that would be likely to occur on the basis of chance alone less than five times out of one hundred, assuming that the sample was drawn at random. Since in our study we are not dealing with a random sample, but rather with a systematic sample of the known and recorded cultures of the world, we cannot say that results that surpass the .05 level are not due to some feature of this systematic sampling process. We therefore use significance levels in our tables as only one aid in culling out patterns in relationships, rather than as the crucial point of reference. We will be as much, or more, interested in the size and signs of the gamma coefficients. In reporting our results we will usually ignore relationships that are statistically significant but nonlinear.

status for women. At the top of each table are listed the independent variables used to test the hypothesis in question, as these were introduced in chapter III. There we also place a row of signs indicating the relationships we expect to find. A plus sign under the name of the independent variable means that positive values of gamma provide support for the hypothesis, while a minus sign indicates that negative gamma values provide such support. In a few tables there are lettered postscripts after some gamma coefficients. These indicate that the coefficient given may be artificially inflated by the influence of another independent variable.[2] These postscripts

2. In separate tests not reported here, we checked for the existence of two potential problems in these results. One we have referred to as Galton's problem, the idea that independent and dependent variables could have diffused together between nearby cultures by historical accident, rather than because of some functional or causal connection between them. To check on the seriousness of this problem in our data, we used a combination of the "interval sift method" and the "linked pair method" described by Naroll (1970b). Since the statistical procedures involved did not substantially reduce any of the associations we will be drawing attention to in the succeeding pages, we concluded that we could ignore Galton's problem in our data.

The second potential problem is one of spurious correlations; the chance that an association between one of our scales and independent variable X might actually be due to the action of another independent variable Y. For example, if we find an association between reliance on hunting and some scale, it might be the case that this association is attributable to the action of a third variable, perhaps the presence or absence of metalworking, which is correlated with that scale. In other words this is a matter of whether each of several independent variables has a strong association with a particular scale in its own right, or whether one or more of the associations involved is an artifact of the other variables. The way to test for this problem is to compute partial associations, controlling one by one for possible spurious factors, and seeing whether our associations are substantially reduced. (Our sample is too small to control for all other possible spurious factors simultaneously.) Where we had several indicators of the same hypothesis, we used the one with the strongest gamma values in these computations, but in indicating problems of spuriousness in our tables we put a lettered postscript after each measure of the same concept. Only in three cases were our associations substantially re-

123

mean that the reader can assume that the "true" association is somewhat weaker than is suggested by the size of the gamma coefficients. Within each table it is the overall pattern of associations we wish to focus on, rather than each individual gamma statistic. In the process some potentially interesting results will be passed over, but we hope thereby to help the reader keep track of the main thrust of our results. Let us proceed, then, to test our original hypotheses one by one.[3]

Hypothesis 1a: Women will have lower relative status in cultures where subsistence is based on intensive plow agriculture than in other cultures.

Clear patterns emerge in table 3 only for four of our scales: domestic authority (DVS 5), ritualized female solidarity (DVS 6), control of sex (DVS 7), and informal influence (DV 52). The first three support our hypothesis—in societies with intensive plow agriculture women tend to have less domestic authority, less ritualized female solidarity, and more unequal restrictions on their sex lives than women in other societies. However, the other scale yields a result opposite to our prediction—in societies with intensive agriculture women are said to have more informal influence than is the case in other societies. (Also in such societies there is a weaker tendency for more joint participaton between

---

duced by controlling for a third variable; in each instance that third variable was region of the world, and in none of these cases did controlling for region eliminate the association completely or reverse the relationship. In other words this indicates that the "real" association between the two variables indicated by our lettered postscripts is weaker than the values of gamma given (due to the spurious action of our region variable), but that it does exist to some extent. Full details on the calculations for both Galton's and spurious correlation problems are available to interested scholars upon request.

3. We note again that our hypotheses are all phrased in terms of "the status of women," while we now realize that no such unitary phenomenon exists. For the sake of simplicity and consistency we have not bothered to change the wording of each hypothesis to reflect the greater complexity we have discovered.

spouses to exist.) The rest of the associations in the table are weak or inconsistent. We will return to these results later when we can place them in the context of our other findings, but already we can see the utility of looking at separate

TABLE 3

TEST OF HYPOTHESIS 1A: INTENSIVE AGRICULTURE—
(Ordinal Gamma Statistics)

	IV 1 Plow	IV 2 Irrigation	IV 3 Grains	IV 4 Roots and Tubers	IV 5 Tree Crops	IV 6 Importance of Agriculture
Expected relationship	—	—	—	+	+	—
DVS 1: Property control	−.22	−.31	−.08	−.29	−.11	.01
DVS 2: Kin power	.37	.32	−.03	−.21	−.36*	−.04
DVS 3: Value of life	−.27	−.26	.04	.06	−.40	−.06
DVS 4: Value of labor	.17	−.01	−.21	.29	.01	.01
DVS 5: Domestic authority	−.55*	−.51*	−.38	.42	.12	−.18
DVS 6: Ritualized female solidarity	−.65*	−.37	−.32	.27	.22	−.19
DVS 7: Control of sex	−.65*	−.49*	−.48*	.17	.69*	−.20*
DVS 8: Ritualized fear	−.32	−.17	−.36	.07	−.32	.03
DVS 9: Joint participation	.07	−.04	.24*	−.09	−.22	.12
DV 52: Informal influence	.51*	.50*	.43*	.11	−.11	.38*
Median N	92	86	92	93	92	93

NOTE: * = relationship likely to occur on basis of chance alone less than five times out of one hundred ($p \leqq .05$).

125

aspects of the role and position of women. Out of our ten measures, five have no strong or consistent relationship with intensive agriculture, three fit our predictions, and one or two yield opposite results. The complexities of these associations would have been lost if we had simply added separate dependent variable scales together, as some earlier scholars did (see Hobhouse, Wheeler, and Ginsburg, 1915, pp. 170-175). By keeping things separate we find evidence that intensive agriculture has some effects on the position of women, but that those effects are rather specific. (Note that in table 3 it is not agriculture in general—see column 6—but specifically intensive plow agriculture that shows the strongest associations.)

Hypothesis 1b: Women will have lower status in cultures where subsistence is based on the herding of large animals than in other cultures.

The associations in table 4 are not as strong or consistent as those in table 3, and they also show that it matters whether domestic animals are indigenous or are a recent introduction (compare columns 4 and 5 with the other columns). For reasons not clear to us, recently introduced animals are associated with some of our scales in a manner almost opposite to our variables for indigenous animals. We chose to focus mainly on the indigenous animals. Four scales show associations similar to those in our previous table: Indigenous herding is associated with less ritualized female solidarity and perhaps with somewhat less domestic authority of women, but with more informal influence exercised by women and perhaps slightly more joint participation of men and women. Thus we conclude that hypothesis 1b is supported for ritualized female solidarity and perhaps domestic authority, contradicted for informal influence and perhaps for joint participation, and not supported for the remaining six scales. This finding conflicts with the earlier report by Hobhouse, Wheeler, and Ginsburg (1915, p. 174) that the status of women is *in general* lower among pastoral peoples.

Hypothesis 1c: Women will have lower status in cultures

126

TABLE 4

TEST OF HYPOTHESIS 1b: ANIMAL HERDING—
(Ordinal Gamma Statistics)

	IV 7 Large Non-milked Domestic animals	IV 8 Large Milked Domestic animals	IV 9 Small Domestic animals	IV 10 Large New Domestic animals	IV 11 Small New Domestic animals	IV 12 Importance of Animal herding
Expected relationship	−	−	−	−	−	−
DVS 1: Property control	.01	−.19	−.06	.36	−.19	−.25
DVS 2: Kin power	.07	−.07	.12	.35	−.17	.05
DVS 3: Value of life	.46	−.47*	−.27	.59	.40	−.15
DVS 4: Value of labor	.22	−.14	−.17	−.24	−.15	−.12
DVS 5: Domestic authority	−.24a	−.46a*	−.48a*	.19	−.08	−.40a*
DVS 6: Ritualized female solidarity	−.13	−.58*	−.34	.48	.54	−.29
DVS 7: Control of sex	−.51	.02	−.24	−.18	.45	−.14
DVS 8: Ritualized fear	.61	−.48	−.25	.01	−.21	−.21
DVS 9: Joint participation	.02	.27	.13	−.39*	−.33	.17
DV 52: Informal influence	.42	.36	.40	−.35	−.08	.33*
Median N	87	90	88	89	81	93

NOTE: a = association weakened when controlled for region of world.

    * = relationship likely to occur on basis of chance alone less than five times out of one hundred ($p \leq .05$).

where subsistence is based on hunting (particularly the hunting of large animals) than in other cultures.

In table 5 our measures of the power of women in kinship realms and the informal influence of women show relationships in the predicted direction; both tend to be lower in

127

TABLE 5

TEST OF HYPOTHESIS 1c: HUNTING—
(Ordinal Gamma Statistics)

	IV 13 Large Animals Hunted	IV 14 Small Animals Hunted	IV 15 Medium Animals Hunted	IV 16 Importance of Hunting and Gathering
Expected relationship	—	—	—	—
DVS 1: Property control	.29	.23	.06	.30
DVS 2: Kin power	−.40	−.26	−.46*	−.12
DVS 3: Value of life	.38a*	.35a	.47a*	.29a
DVS 4: Value of labor	.01	−.12	.08	.06
DVS 5: Domestic authority	.59*	.31	.35	.42*
DVS 6: Ritualized female solidarity	.52*	.45*	.65*	.51*
DVS 7: Control of sex	−.06	−.24	.07	.10
DVS 8: Ritualized fear	.21	.04	.28	.05
DVS 9: Joint participation	−.06	−.03	.02	−.14
DV 52: Informal influence	−.33	−.29	−.37	−.36
Median N	86	82	82	93

NOTE: a = association weakened when controlled for region of world.

* = relationship likely to occur on basis of chance alone less than five times out of one hundred ($p \leq .05$).

hunting societies. Yet five of our other scales show relationships of varying strength in a direction opposite to our predictions. In hunting societies in comparison with other societies, women have more domestic authority, more ritualized solidarity, and perhaps also more value placed on their lives, more control over property, and less ritualized fear from

128

men. (Note also that the associations with our indicators of the hunting of large animals and medium-sized animals generally are stronger than those with our indicator of the hunting of small animals.) Thus contrary to our original prediction, on balance hunting seems to be associated with more benefits for women than disadvantages. We can't be certain how much the hunting way of life of cultures in our sample is like the life of the hunters in our own evolutionary past, but this pattern of findings throws considerable doubt on any notion that the nature of the male role in hunting produces selective pressures for male domination of women. In a number of important ways contemporary hunting societies show more egalitarian relations between the sexes than do other societies.

Hypothesis 2a: Women will have lower status in cultures with constant warfare than in other cultures.

Hypothesis 2b: Women will have higher status in cultures with constant warfare than in other cultures.

In table 6 we have only one independent variable to work with, which deprives us of the opportunity to examine patterns across several different indicators of our hypothesis. We see one association in the table that supports hypothesis 2a: in cultures with frequent warfare there is less joint social life between men and women. However, most of the signs in the table are positive, indicating more support for hypothesis 2b. The strongest associations tell us that in cultures with frequent warfare women have more domestic authority, somewhat more ritualized solidarity, and perhaps more value placed on their lives.

This last relationship, although modest in size, is important to note because many ethological speculations current these days assume that when men spend much of their time in warfare they will also tend to brutalize their women. Our value of life scale (DVS 3) includes an item for whether husbands are encouraged to beat their wives, but in fact we find that women are treated somewhat *better*, with wife beating not encouraged, in cultures with frequent warfare than in other cultures.

129

TABLE 6

TEST OF HYPOTHESES 2a AND 2b: WARFARE— AND WARFARE+
(Ordinal Gamma Statistics)

Expected relationship	IV 17 Frequency of Intercommunity Warfare −(2a) or +(2b)
DVS 1: Property control	.09
DVS 2: Kin power	.01
DVS 3: Value of life	.27
DVS 4: Value of labor	.07
DVS 5: Domestic authority	.44*
DVS 6: Ritualized female solidarity	.36
DVS 7: Control of sex	.14
DVS 8: Ritualized fear	−.22
DVS 9: Joint participation	−.45*
DV 52: Informal influence	−.09
Median N:	91

NOTE: * = relationship likely to occur on basis of chance alone less than five times out of one hundred ($p \leq .05$).

If we compare the pattern of our findings thus far, it will be apparent that something is wrong with the argument that the greater strength and aggressiveness of the male is the crucial element in the domination of women. All of the hypotheses examined so far, with the exception of 2b, take the following logical form: Activity X requires much strength, stamina, or aggressiveness. Since men tend to have more of these qualities than women, activity X will be performed primarily by men. Therefore in cultures where activity X is particularly important, men will use their monopoly over that activity to gain in status relative to women. (The same logical pattern can be used with our alternative explanation, that women are disqualified from such activities on the basis of their childbearing burden.) Within this logical pattern we have substituted plowing, herding of large animals, hunting, and warfare for X. If the reasoning behind the pattern were correct, we would expect to find a similar pattern of results in tables 3-6 (with the exception of the test of hypothesis 2b). Yet this is not the case. The pattern of associations for hunting and warfare is quite different from, and some ways almost the opposite of, the pattern that emerges for intensive agriculture and herding. One common underlying mechanism, such as the importance of male strength or women's childbearing burdens, cannot explain such divergent patterns. Whatever dominance men achieve in plowing and herding societies cannot be explained by the fact that the subsistence activities involved require great strength, stamina, or mobility. We are left with a puzzle. We have discovered some fairly strong associations, but our original explanation does not fit the pattern of those relationships. In succeeding pages we will have to look for some other mechanism that can account for our divergent findings in tables 3-4 and 5-6.

Hypothesis 3: In cultures with a high degree of institutionalized male solidarity, women will have lower status than in other cultures.

We have two variables to test this hypothesis, and the results are consistently negative. There is no tendency for institutionalized male solidarity to be associated with either benefits or disadvantages for women.[4] We can therefore reject hypothesis 3 entirely. Together with our findings on hunt-

4. This negative finding is particularly puzzling for DVS 6, our measure of ritualized sexual separation. Young found (Young 1965; Young and Bacdayan, 1965) that male solidarity (in the form of such things as male initiation rites and men's houses) was part of a larger concept of "social rigidity" that, as we have indicated earlier, includes also separate women's solidarity, in forms such as the female initiation rites that are part of DVS 6. For reasons that are not entirely clear to us our measures of male solidarity and of ritualized sexual separation, which seem to concern the same things as Young and Bacdayan's social rigidity, although measured somewhat differently, are not associated with one another cross-culturally in our sample. We have already drawn attention to the fact that our measure of ritualized seuxal separation (DVS 6) also does not have the negative connotations for women that Young and Bacdayan saw for their related concept. Further research will be needed to explain these conflicting findings.

TABLE 7

TEST OF HYPOTHESIS 3: MALE SOLIDARITY—
(Ordinal Gamma Statistics)

	IV 18 Male Initiation Ceremonies	IV 19 Male Solidarity
Expected relationship	—	—
DVS 1: Property control	.25	—.06
DVS 2: Kin power	—.08	—.07
DVS 3: Value of life	.02	.07
DVS 4: Value of labor	.27	—.00
DVS 5: Domestic authority	.31	.16
DVS 6: Ritualized female solidarity	.03	.02
DVS 7: Control of sex	—.02	—.09
DVS 8: Ritualized fear	—.17	—.23
DVS 9: Joint participation	.02	—.34
DV 52: Informal influence	—.14	—.02
Median N	75	93

NOTE: * = relationship likely to occur on basis of chance alone less than five times out of one hundred ($p \leq .05$).

ing and warfare, we are led also to reject the chain of evolutionary causation proposed by Lionel Tiger and discussed
in chapter III—that early hunting led to male bonding, and
that male bonding in turn led to male domination of women.
Neither hunting nor male bonding seems to be associated
with male domination.

Hypothesis 4a: In cultures with matrilineal descent, women
will have higher status than in other cultures.

Hypothesis 4b: In cultures with matrilocal postmarital
residence rules, women will have higher status than in other
cultures.

Here there is only one relationship that is particularly
strong, but several others of consistent sign and modest size.
The clearest pattern is for women in matrilineal and matrilocal cultures to have more control over property than women

TABLE 8

TEST OF HYPOTHESES 4a: MATRILINEAL DESCENT+,
AND OF 4b: MATRILOCAL RESIDENCE+
(Ordinal Gamma Statistics)

	IV 20 Descent	IV 21 Postmarital Residence
Expected relationship	+	+
DVS 1: Property control	.59*	.65*
DVS 2: Kin power	—.25	.02
DVS 3: Value of life	.29a	.52a
DVS 4: Value of labor	—.13	.37
DVS 5: Domestic authority	.24	.25
DVS 6: Ritualized female solidarity	.25	.42
DVS 7: Control of sex	.26	.29
DVS 8: Ritualized fear	.16	—.02
DVS 9: Joint participation	.14	.01
DV 52: Informal influence	.16	—.20
Median N:	93	90

NOTE: a = association weakened when controlled for region of world.

* = relationship likely to occur on basis of chance alone less than five times out of one hundred ($p \leq .05$).

in other cultures, but the weaker patterns show women in such societies with somewhat more domestic authority, more ritualized female solidarity, more equal sexual restrictions, and perhaps more value placed on their lives. We do not find a consistent relationship with the relative value of the labor of women, although some existing studies led us to expect it.[5] The best general summation of table 8 is that, in

5. Some work on kinship systems suggests that a change in subsistence activities toward forms engaged in mostly by women (e.g., certain kinds of horticulture) is often followed by a change in residence rules to matrilocal residence, which may in turn lead to a shift to matrilineal descent—all in order to facilitate social ties among the primary producers, the women (see Steward, 1955; Murdock, 1949).

133

keeping with the writings cited earlier by Murdock, Gough, and Schlegel, matrilineal descent and matrilocal residence are associated with certain benefits for women. However, with the exception of control over property, these benefits are not very powerful.

Hypothesis 5: Women have lower status in cultures that favor large extended families than in cultures that favor nuclear families.

TABLE 9

TEST OF HYPOTHESIS 5: EXTENDED FAMILIES— (Ordinal Gamma Statistics)

	IV 22 Preferred Family Form
Expected relationship	—
DVS 1: Property control	—.08
DVS 2: Kin power	—.03
DVS 3: Value of life	—.02
DVS 4: Value of labor	—.04
DVS 5: Domestic authority	—.20
DVS 6: Ritualized female solidarity	—.07
DVS 7: Control of sex	—.07
DVS 8: Ritualized fear	—.11
DVS 9: Joint participation	.01
DV 52: Informal influence	—.03
Median N:	88

NOTE: * = relationship likely to occur on basis of chance alone less than five times out of one hundred $(p \leq .05)$.

Our results do not give much support to this argument, although we do find the value of women's labor more closely connected with residence rules than with descent. Ember and Ember (1971) have produced evidence that other factors, particularly the nature of local warfare, are more important in determining residence rules than is the nature of subsistence activities.

134

We see in table 9 that the predicted relationship between extended family forms and the subordination of women is not borne out for any of our scales. The argument on which this hypothesis was based (greater internal family hierarchy and more narrow division of labor favoring males) can therefore be rejected. Perhaps in extended families women as well as men in the older generation gain in authority by having more family members to control, thus acquiring competencies that may compensate for a rigid division of labor in the economic realm. (An alternative explanation would focus on the fact that, even in those preindustrial societies favoring extended families, most people spend much of their lives in nuclear arrangements—see Coale, 1965. Thus the mechanism assumed by hypothesis 5 would not operate very widely or have much influence.)

Hypothesis 6: Women will have lower status in cultures with complex political hierarchies such as the state or an autocratic kingdom than in other cultures.

Three sets of relationships in this table are fairly strong and consistent. In cultures with complex political structures women do, as predicted, have less domestic authority and less ritualized solidarity with other women. Contrary to our original prediction, women in such cultures also have somewhat more informal influence than women in other cultures. This finding adds to our suspicions that our informal influence item is dealing with something not so beneficial for women—perhaps their lack of *formal* power and influence. Weaker associations in the predicted direction are visible for two other scales: women in politically complex societies have slightly less control over property and more unequal sexual restrictions placed on them than is the case in other societies. The pattern we have found in testing hypothesis 6 is quite similar to the one we noted in examining intensive agriculture and animal husbandry (in tables 3 and 4). This tells us that there may be a common factor underlying both sets of relationships, an idea we will pursue further shortly.

135

TABLE 10

Test of Hypothesis 6: Political Hierarchy—
(Ordinal Gamma Statistics)

	IV 23 Political Organization	IV 24 Crimes Punished	IV 25 Government Bureaucrats	IV 26 Present Kingdom	IV 27 Past Kingdom
Expected relationship	—	—	—	—	—
DVS 1: Property control	—.25	—.12	—.22	—.38	—.04
DVS 2: Kin power	.08	—.04	.07	—.37	.22
DVS 3: Value of life	—.12	—.20	—.12	.06	—.23
DVS 4: Value of labor	—.11	—.16	—.01	—.27	.26
DVS 5: Domestic authority	—.28	—.29	—.67*	—.38	—.20
DVS 6: Ritualized female solidarity	—.36*	—.44*	—.36	—.14	—.49
DVS 7: Control of sex	—.19	—.07	—.18	—.14	—.20
DVS 8: Ritualized fear	—.23	—.01	—.07	—.30	.12
DVS 9: Joint participation	.09	—.14	.05	.45	—.07
DV 52: Informal influence	.54*	.56*	.63*	.36	.46
Median N:	91	92	92	87	87

NOTE: * = relationship likely to occur on basis of chance alone less than five time
out of one hundred ($p \leq .05$).

Hypothesis 7: Women will have lower status in cultures possessing significant private property rights in the means of production than in cultures lacking the same.

In table 11 there is only one really strong relationship—with less value of the labor of women where private property rights exist—but several other weaker relationships are

TABLE 11

TEST OF HYPOTHESIS 7: PRIVATE PROPERTY—
(Ordinal Gamma Statistics)

	IV 28 *Private Property*
Expected relationship	—
DVS 1: Property control	−.39
DVS 2: Kin power	−.16
DVS 3: Value of life	−.27
DVS 4: Value of labor	−.67*
DVS 5: Domestic authority	−.17
DVS 6: Ritualized female solidarity	−.00
DVS 7: Control of sex	−.51
DVS 8: Ritualized fear	−.39
DVS 9: Joint participation	.11
DV 52: Informal influence	.43
Median N:	84

NOTE: * = relationship likely to occur on basis of chance alone less than five times out of one hundred ($p \leq .05$).

in the predicted direction. We note modest tendencies for societies with private property to also have unequal sexual restrictions, less property rights for women, more ritualized fear of women, but *more* informal influence by women (again the contrary pattern for this item). Thus there may be a modest tendency in cultures with private property for women to have somewhat lower status or more restricted roles in some areas of social life than in other cultures. The figures in table 11 do not lead us to believe, however, that the advent of private property is in some sense *the* crucial change affecting women, given the modest size of the figures involved.

Hypothesis 8: In more complex and differentiated cultures women will have lower status than in less complex cultures.

In order to test hypothesis 8 we have brought together in table 12 a wide variety of variables that we can relate di-

137

TABLE 12

TEST OF HYPOTHESIS 8: SOCIETAL COMPLEXITY—
(Ordinal Gamma Statistics)

	Plow (IV 1)	Irrigation (IV 2)	Grains (IV 3)	Importance of Agriculture (IV 6)	Political Organization (IV 23)	Private Property (IV 28)	Settlement Size (IV 29)	Metal-working (IV 30)	Pottery Making (IV 31)	Weaving (IV 32)	Societal Stratification (IV 33)	Community Stratification (IV 34)	Societal Complexity (IV 35)
Expected relationship	—	—	—	—	—	—	—	—	—	—	—	—	—
DVS 1: Property control	-.22	-.31	-.08	.01	-.25	-.39	-.04	-.02	-.23	-.10	-.18	-.15	-.04*
DVS 2: Kin power	.37	.32	-.03	-.04	.08	-.16	.04	-.01	-.16	.18	.11	.20	.12
DVS 3: Value of life	-.27	-.26	.04	-.06	-.12	-.27	-.09	.07	.17	-.04	-.04	-.02	-.16
DVS 4: Value of labor	.17	-.01	-.21	.01	-.11	-.67*	-.06	-.12	-.02	-.11	-.10	-.08	-.07
DVS 5: Domestic authority	-.55*	-.51*	-.38	-.18	-.28	-.17	-.22	-.14	-.02	-.55*	-.36	-.40	-.32*
DVS 6: Ritualized female solidarity	-.65*	-.37	-.32	-.19	-.36*	-.00	-.28	-.02	.17	-.39*	-.33*	-.31	-.40*
DVS 7: Control of sex	-.65*	-.49*	-.48*	-.20*	-.19	-.51	-.40	-.11	-.05	-.65*	-.28	-.55*	-.11
DVS 8: Ritualized fear	-.32	-.17	-.36	.03	-.23	-.39	-.01	-.05	-.39	-.08	-.18	-.21	-.02*
DVS 9: Joint participation	.07	-.04	.24*	.12	.09	.11	-.01	.19	-.22	.23	.31*	.35*	-.08
DV 52: Informal influence	.51*	.50*	.43*	.38*	.54*	.43	.43*	.56*	.52*	.35*	.51*	.42	.53*
Median N:	92	86	92	93	91	84	90	86	90	86	92	90	93

NOTE: * = relationship likely to occur on basis of chance along less than five times out of one hundred ($p \leq .05$).

rectly to our general concept of societal complexity. Some of these variables have already been used in testing earlier hypotheses. The figures in table 12 provide fairly consistent support for hypothesis 8 for three scales. In more complex societies women tend to have less domestic authority, less ritualized solidarity, and more unequal sexual restrictions. Examination of the pattern of these relationships with our technological items reveals weaker associations with metal-working and pottery than with weaving, irrigation, and the plow. Since these technological items tend to occur at different evolutionary levels, with pottery making and metalworking generally much earlier than the other three items,[6] we have reason to suspect that the most important evolutionary transition for women is between societies of intermediate and high complexity (high in terms of the limits of our sample), rather than between societies of low and intermediate complexity. Thus, for example, the shift from subsistence based on hunting and gathering to one based on shifting or extensive agriculture (horticulture) seems to be less important than the further shift to intensive, plow agriculture. Yet the pattern of associations in table 12 is sufficiently general that it is hard to say what specific aspect of complexity is most important—that in politics, technology, stratification, or

6. In our sample the number of cultures coded present on these five indicators was as follows: pottery—64/93, metalworking—51/93, weaving—43/93, irrigation—31/93, and the plow—25/93. Subsequently we found that these five items could be made into a Guttman scale of technological complexity (coefficient of scalability = .72), which has a correlation of $r = .65$ with our scale of societal complexity (IV 35). In other words there is clear evidence that these technological innovations occur cross-culturally in the order given. In this study we use the original five items rather than the combined scale. Two of the relationships with our general societal complexity scale (IV 35) show low gammas, but surpass our significance level, indicating a curvilinear relationship. Examination of the contingency tables (not reproduced here) shows that in societies judged as intermediate in complexity women have more control over property and receive less ritualized fear from men than they do in either the simplest or most complex societies in our sample.

139

some other area. Perhaps the technology and social organization associated with intensive agriculture is somewhat more important than the type of stratification, which is in turn somewhat more important than the form of political organization. However, all of these aspects of complexity seem to be interwoven and in some general fashion to affect the lot of women.

Two other scales in table 12 show weaker associations in the predicted direction—in more complex societies women have somewhat less control over property and receive more ritualized fear from men. Three other scales in the table show negligible or inconsistent associations with indicators of complexity, but our final two scales show patterns opposite to those predicted. In more complex societies there is somewhat more joint participation of men and women in social life, and women tend strongly to have more informal influence than women in other cultures have. Again we are led to suspect that this informal influence is some sort of compensation or reaction to the increasing restrictions placed on the formal authority of women.

We now feel that we have an explanation for our findings on hypotheses 1a-2a, dealing with agriculture, herding, hunting, and warfare. Intensive agriculture and herding are subsistence activities that tend to be emphasized in complex societies (within our sample), while hunting and intercommunity warfare are more important in simpler societies. It seems to be the complexity and not the importance of male strength or some similar factor that explains why things such as the domestic authority, ritual solidarity, sexual regulations, and informal influence of women vary. We still have not explained *why* complexity should have these effects (recall that our discussion of hypothesis 8 in chapter III was rather vague), and we will return to this task after we consider the results of tests of our other hypotheses.[7]

7. Another puzzle in our findings is that, if complexity is systematically related to some of our scales, why wasn't our family form variable in table 9 also related to them, since a number of studies

Hypothesis 9: Women will have lower status in cultures where classical religions are practiced (e.g., Christianity, Islam, Hinduism, Buddhism) than in cultures with pre-classical religions.

TABLE 13

TEST OF HYPOTHESIS 9: CLASSICAL RELIGION—
(Ordinal Gamma Statistics)

	IV 36 Type of Religion
Expected relationship	—
DVS 1: Property control	—.19
DVS 2: Kin power	.18
DVS 3: Value of life	—.05
DVS 4: Value of labor	.04
DVS 5: Domestic authority	—.27
DVS 6: Ritualized female solidarity	—.49*
DVS 7: Control of sex	.01
DVS 8: Ritualized fear	—.20
DVS 9: Joint participation	—.08
DV 52: Informal influence	.42
Median N:	93

NOTE: * = relationship likely to occur on basis of chance alone less than five times out of one hundred ($p \leq .05$).

cited earlier (Nimkoff and Middleton, 1960; Blumberg and Winch, 1972) claim that family structure itself is related to the general level of societal complexity, with extended families found most often in complex societies based upon intensive agriculture. We looked into the issue and found that within our sample, our measure of family structure (IV 22) had no strong and consistent relationship with various measures of societal complexity. We also located other studies in the literature (see Osmond, 1969) that disagree with the claimed relationship between societal complexity and extended families. Given this lack of a family complexity/general complexity connection in our data, it is quite understandable that complexity can be related to our dependent variables scales while our family form measure is not.

141

In this table we see only two strong associations. In cultures with classical religions in comparison with other cultures women are less likely to have ritualized solidarity with other women emphasized, and they are more likely to use informal influence to get their way. Classical religions are, of course, more often found in relatively complex cultures (the correlation between IV 35 and IV 36 is $r = .56$), so we had to check whether the two strong associations in table 13 are an artifact of complexity in general. Statistical controls for general complexity (not reported here) did not substantially reduce the size of these two associations; therefore we conclude that the type of religion has an independent effect on ritualized female solidarity and women's informal influence. (Conversely, the associations of these and other scales with societal complexity are not simply produced by the fact that complex societies tend to have classical religions practiced in them, religions whose doctrines restrict the role of women.) Looked at in another way, these findings indicate that some part of the distinctive position of women in complex societies can be carried into less complex societies as a result of missionary activity and conversion to classical religions.

Hypothesis 10a: Low status of women is associated with a high degree of institutionalized envy between the sexes.

Hypothesis 10b: High status of women is associated with a high degree of institutionalized envy between the sexes.

Here we can see that neither version of the "sexual envy" hypothesis is supported. Even our ritualized female solidarity and ritualized fear scales, which both have to do with separation and perhaps antagonism between men and women, do not provide clear support. If there is any substance to the arguments underlying these status envy hypotheses, the effects are too subtle for our single rough scale to detect.

Hypothesis 11a: Women will have higher status in cultures where there is a shortage of women than in other cultures.

142

TABLE 14

TEST OF HYPOTHESES 10a AND 10b: INSTITUTIONALIZED ENVY— OR +
(Ordinal Gamma Statistics)

	IV 37 *Institutionalized Envy*
Expected relationship	—(10a) or +(10b)
DVS 1: Property control	.08
DVS 2: Kin power	—.08
DVS 3: Value of life	—.04
DVS 4: Value of labor	—.06
DVS 5: Domestic authority	.19
DVS 6: Ritualized female solidarity	—.02
DVS 7: Control of sex	—.10
DVS 8: Ritualized fear	—.21
DVS 9: Joint participation	.30
DV 52: Informal influence	.02
Median N:	86

NOTE: * = relationship likely to occur on basis of chance alone less than five times
out of one hundred ($p \leq .05$).

Hypothesis 11b: Women will have higher status in cultures where men are absent for long periods of time than in other cultures.

Again we see no support for our hypotheses in table 15, and in fact the signs in the table are more often than not the opposite of those expected. For example, a shortage of women is not associated with more value being placed on the lives of women, as predicted, but somewhat the reverse. In retrospect this makes some sense, since one of the items in DVS 3 deals with female infanticide. Where this occurs widely, other things being equal, women are obviously going to be in short supply. In general we can conclude that none of our scales supports the hypotheses dealing with the influence of demographic factors. We should also recall that

TABLE 15

TEST OF HYPOTHESES 11a: FEMALE SHORTAGE+
AND OF 11b: MALE ABSENCE+
(Ordinal Gamma Statistics)

	IV 38 Sex Ratio	IV 39 Male Absence
Expected relationship	+	+
DVS 1: Property control	—.06	—.07
DVS 2: Kin power	.07	.22
DVS 3: Value of life	—.44	—.20
DVS 4: Value of labor	—.01	—.17
DVS 5: Domestic authority	—.02	—.20
DVS 6: Ritualized female solidarity	—.14	—.20
DVS 7: Control of sex	—.08	—.27
DVS 8: Ritualized fear	—.04	.06
DVS 9: Joint participation	—.11	—.16
DV 52: Informal influence	—.04	.06
Median N:	90	92

NOTE: * = relationship likely to occur on basis of chance alone less than five times
out of one hundred ($p \leq .05$).

the reasoning underlying hypothesis 11b was also used initially in presenting hypothesis 2b—when men are absent for
long periods, such as when engaging in frequent warfare,
women will gain in importance. Since hypothesis 11b has now
been refuted, we must conclude that male absence did not
explain the partial support we found earlier for hypothesis 2b,
our indicator of the "Rosie-the-riveter" phenomenon. We
feel that the partial benefits women receive in cultures with
frequent intercommunity warfare are attributable not to male
absence, but to the fact that such cultures tend to be at the
low end on our various complexity measures.[8]

8. It is important to note that these statements refer to intercommunity warfare, and not warfare in general. We do not claim that
more complex societies have less warfare, only that their centralized
political institutions suppress fighting between communities and con-

Now we come to a set of hypothesized relationships between our scales and particular "crucial" dependent variables. In table 16 we of course omit figures on associations between such a variable and any scale that contains that variable as one of its included items.

Hypothesis 12: The greater the control women have over the valuable property in a culture, the higher will be their general status.

Hypothesis 13: In cultures where women are organized collectively for economic activities their general status will be higher than in other cultures.

Hypothesis 14a: In cultures where women contribute much to subsistence, there general status will be higher than where women contribute little.

Hypothesis 14b: In cultures where women contribute much to subsistence, their general status will be lower than where they contribute little.

Hypothesis 15: In cultures where women have substantial control over the fruits of productive labor their general status will be higher than where they have little control.

Hypothesis 16: In cultures with a great deal of polygyny women will have lower status in general than in cultures with preferential monogamy or polyandry.

The relationships in table 16 are generally very weak. Perhaps we can say that there is some relationship between women's control over the fruits of labor and less ritualized fear of women by men and with greater domestic authority for women. We also note that the signs of our associations with marriage form (column 6) are generally opposite to our prediction, indicating some slight *benefits* where polygyny is practiced. However, the rest of the matrix lacks a consistent pattern of relationships. We expect in a table of this size, on

---

duct warfare on the basis of specially recruited military forces against primarily external enemies (see S. Andreski, 1968). Thus warfare may be more frequent or more important in these more complex societies, but will engage less of the time and energies of the average villager.

TABLE 16

TESTS OF HYPOTHESES 12-16: THE INFLUENCE OF KEY DEPENDENT VARIABLES
(Ordinal Gamma Statistics)

	IV 40 Inheritance Rights	IV 41 Women's Work Groups	IV 42 Women's Subsistence Contribution	IV 43 Fruits of Male Labor	IV 44 Fruits of Joint Labor	IV 45 Fruits of Female Labor	IV 46 Marriage Form
Expected relationship	+	+	+(14a) or −(14b)	+	+	+	+
DVS 1: Property control	X	−.12	.34	X	X	X	−.03
DVS 2: Kin power	.18	−.51*	−.16	.13	−.07	−.04	X
DVS 3: Value of life	.35	.37	.18	−.14	−.02	−.03	−.14
DVS 4: Value of labor	−.03	−.16	X	.14	.17	−.24	.10
DVS 5: Domestic authority	.27	−.07	.00	.24	.54*	.39	−.06
DVS 6: Ritualized female solidarity	.27	X	−.01	−.04	−.01	.05	−.27
DVS 7: Control of sex	−.15	.53	.13	−.23	−.24	.08	−.02
DVS 8: Ritualized fear	.37	.04	.08	.24*	.24*	.36	−.03
DVS 9: Joint participation	.06	−.24	.06	.05	−.13	−.04	−.18
DV 52: Informal influence	−.16	.34	.12	.13	.02	.01	−.18
Median N:	71	72	89	92	81	92	93

NOTE: X = IV is part of dependent variable scale, test not appropriate.

* = relationship likely to occur on basis of chance alone less than five times out of one hundred ($p \leq .05$).

the basis of chance alone, to find 3.15 significant associations, and we find only 4. With these few possible exceptions, we reject hypotheses 12-16 on the basis of these data.[9] This is not really surprising, since these results simply reaffirm the conclusions of chapter V. There we found that aspects of the status, roles, and relationship of the sexes used in this study are largely independent of each other, and that there is no particular aspect of the status of women that, if known, will allow one to predict how women will stand on other measures. Thus we should not expect to find some "crucial" feature of the role of women that affects all others. To understand why the position of women varies around the world, we need to turn not to some such crucial feature, but to the overall ways in which societies are organized, people conduct their religious life, and so forth.

We have now concluded consideration of our primary

9. This result contradicts the conclusions of two earlier cross-cultural studies that used smaller and more limited samples. In a pilot study using only 12 cultures, Sanday (1974) claimed that a general scale of female status *could* be constructed, and that this scale had a *curvilinear* relationship with a measure of the proportional subsistence contribution of women, with women having the highest status in cultures where work was shared equally by both sexes. We, of course, found no such general scale of female status, and our proportional subsistence measure had no relationship, curvilinear or otherwise, with any of our separate scales dealing with the status, roles, and relationship of the sexes. (A curvilinear relationship would not be detectable from our gamma coefficients, but would have shown itself in the contingency tables and by significant values of chi-square statistics.) Sacks (1971, 1974), using a sample of four African cultures, concluded that women's control of family property is a primary determinant of their domestic authority, at least in societies without clearly demarcated social classes, and that collective women's work organizations have an important influence on the status of women outside of the family. In columns 1 and 2 of table 14 we can see that in our sample neither variable has the kind of importance Sacks claims they should. Our failure to replicate the findings of these studies indicates to us the danger of building theories about the place of women in social life on the basis of limited and noncomprehensive samples of cultures.

147

hypotheses. Yet we must still deal with the possibility that our results are artifacts of problems in our sources or in our coding, rather than reflections of social dynamics in the cultures themselves. Our technique here is identical with that used in considering the previous hypotheses, only now we use our quality control variables CV 1-CV 11.

Hypothesis 17: Variation in the relative status of women in our sample is an artifact produced by problems in our sources and in our data collection techniques.

From table 17 we can see that the quality control problems in our data are not especially serious. None of the control variables affects our scales in a strong and consistent manner. We expect to find 5.5 significant relationships in a table of this size on the basis of chance alone, and there are only 5 observed. One of these relatively strong associations concerns the variable most often identified in the literature as a source of serious bias, the sex of the authorities who studied a particular culture (CV 5). The fact that men rather than women were the observers of particular cultures may underestimate the control over property that women have in such cultures, but otherwise the sex of the authority does not seem very important. In spite of the generally low associations in table 17 we conducted tests to determine whether any of the results reported in previous tables could be artifacts of the quality of our sources (as indicated by the five significant associations in this table). None of these tests (which we do not report here) substantially reduce the associations uncovered earlier, and we conclude that we can reject hypothesis 17. Variation in aspects of the status, roles, and relationship of the sexes in our data is not simply an artifact of these data quality problems.

We pause here to comment on the significance of this rejection of hypothesis 17. One issue a cross-cultural study dealing with women must address is whether it is even possible to get reliable cross-cultural data on the role of women. The negative argument goes something like this: Most anthro-

148

TABLE 17
TEST OF HYPOTHESIS 17: DATA QUALITY+
(Ordinal Gamma Statistics)

Expected relationship	CV 1 Sex of Coders +	CV 2 Number of Sources +	CV 3 Number of Authorities +	CV 4 Number of Pages +	CV 5 Sex of Authorities +	CV 6 Nationality +?	CV 7 Occupation +	CV 8 Fieldwork Training +	CV 9 Knowledge of Language +	CV 10 Length of Fieldwork +	CV 11 Anthropological Present +
DVS 1: Property control	−.11	.22	.19	.07	.41*	−.21	.04	.04	.21	−.08	.01
DVS 2: Kin power	−.10	.17	.27	.05	−.06	.01	.15	.15	.19	−.05	−.13
DVS 3: Value of life	−.15	−.02	.06	.14	.15	.06	−.29	−.24	−.12	.18	−.32
DVS 4: Value of labor	.14	.09	.13	.02	−.06	−.05	.10	.14	.04	−.00	.14
DVS 5: Domestic authority	−.04	.10	.14	−.15	.20	−.33	.03	.12	−.40	−.08	−.01
DVS 6: Ritualized female solidarity	−.16	−.22	−.20	.03	−.10	.15	−.35	−.34	−.29*	−.04	−.21
DVS 7: Control of sex	.04	−.07	−.12	.21	−.08	.46*	−.21	−.20	.44*	.30	.01
DVS 8: Ritualized fear	.13	.20	.15	.16	.28	−.22	.07	.07	.23	.15	.08
DVS 9: Joint participation	.04	.12	.03	−.23	.05	−.05	.12	.12	−.24	−.14	−.08
DV 52: Informal influence	.25	−.06	.05	.33	.24	.23*	−.10	−.05	−.03	.19	.29
Median N:	93	93	93	93	93	93	91	92	87	89	93

NOTE: * = relationship likely to occur on basis of chance alone less than five times out of one hundred ($p \leq .05$).

pologists have been males and have reported on cultures they studied with a male bias. Fieldworkers, perhaps especially the Americans, also have suffered from a "bourgeois" bias, feeling that the proper place for women is in the home. This has led them to underreport the public role of women. Aspects of the role of women that have not fit the male, bourgeois preconceptions of fieldworkers get ignored. Women fieldworkers generally have been trained by men and have also been influenced by such biases. Therefore until fieldworkers with a feminist eye can restudy the world's cultures, it will not be possible to conduct a cross-cultural study dealing adequately with the role of women.

Whatever the logical merits of this argument (and there are problems even in this regard),[10] if we accept it at face value we should still expect some studies to show more or less male or bourgeois bias than others. Studies done by women, by non-Americans, by more recent fieldworkers, or by people who spent longer in the field should yield more accurate pictures of the role of women. If greater accuracy means reporting a better or more important role for women in social life, such biases should show up in table 17. Yet table 17 provides no evidence for such systematic biases. The figures there do not prove that the depiction of women's roles in all of our sources is full and accurate, devoid of any biases. They only show that such biases tend to have a random, rather than a systematic, effect upon our results. The differences in our scales cannot be explained away as the results of male or bourgeois biases. Thus we feel safe in reporting

10. One counterargument is that anthropologists have always been primarily oriented toward the novel and exotic. They have seen their role as portraying to the world things that are distinctive and odd about the cultures they study, an orientation that may incline them to exaggerate rather than ignore the ways in which the role of women in these other cultures differs from that in which the fieldworker was reared. Thus the nondomestic roles of women may receive special attention, while their domestic role is felt to be too familiar to deserve notice.

150

our findings even before the future generation of feminist
field studies becomes available.[11]

Hypothesis 18: Variation in the relative status of women
in our sample is an artifact produced by simple regional
variation and the patterns of historical diffusion of cultural
traits.

TABLE 18

TEST OF HYPOTHESIS 18: THE INFLUENCE OF
WORLD REGIONS
(Nominal Chi-Square Statistics)

	CV 12 Region of the World
DVS 1: Property control	9.1
DVS 2: Kin power	17.6
DVS 3: Value of life	23.8*
DVS 4: Value of labor	23.8
DVS 5: Domestic authority	27.3*
DVS 6: Ritualized female solidarity	25.5*
DVS 7: Control of sex	15.8
DVS 8: Ritualized fear	13.1
DVS 9: Joint participation	10.3
DV 52: Informal influence	10.6
Median N:	93

NOTE: * = relationship likely to occur on basis of chance alone less
than five times out of one hundred ($p \le .05$).

Earlier in this chapter we noted that separate tests for diffusion effects (the so-called Galton's problem) found them
to be of negligible importance in our data. However, we still

11. Our argument does not mean that having more women as fieldworkers is undesirable or unimportant. We accept the view that
women fieldworkers may be able to uncover fuller and more accurate
information about the role of women in the cultures they study than
men can. However, we doubt that this more accurate picture will
consistently be one in which women have a loftier position than that
portrayed in studies by male fieldworkers (see Whyte, 1978b).

need to examine whether there are systematic differences in regions of the world in our measures of the position of women. In table 18 we' do not use the statistic gamma, which is appropriate only for variables that are logically ordered (which our six regions of the world are not). Instead we report the values of the chi-square statistic. In table 18 we can see that there are important regional variations in several of our scales. In general these are cases in which higher scale scores occur most often in North and South American cultures and least often in the circum-Mediterranean area and in east Eurasia. Since cultures in the latter two areas tend to be more complex than those elsewhere in our sample, we have to examine whether some of our previous findings in regard to complexity can be attributed simply to the difference among world regions, irrespective of the organization of the cultures within those regions. We examined our previous findings while controlling statistically for regions of the world. We found in three cases that individual associations were weakened—those between animal herding and women's domestic authority, between hunting and the type of residence, and between descent and the value placed on women's lives (see tables 4, 5, and 8). These controls did not eliminate these relationships entirely, and other associations were unaffected by this control for region. At the same time, controls for various complexity variables did not eliminate the fairly strong associations between world regions and our scales for the value of women's lives, their domestic authority, and the ritualized solidarity of women. We can summarize these results by saying that there are clear regional differences for at least three of our dependent variable scales, but that region variation alone cannot explain the findings of previous tables. Both societal complexity and region of the world have independent effects on some of our dependent variable scales. Looked at once again in another way, this means that some of the distinctiveness of the lot of women in complex societies exists in, and perhaps has been

152

spread to, some of the simpler societies that are located in regions where complex societies are particularly concentrated.

Given the large number of hypotheses and variables used in this study it becomes difficult, as the reader has no doubt discovered, to keep the results in mind. To aid in summarizing what we have found, we add a final table in which the columns are our individual hypotheses and the rows are our ten dependent variable scales. Where we have judged a hypothesis confirmed for a particular scale, we have entered a + at the appropriate point in the matrix, with a 0 when the hypothesis is not supported and a − where the hypothesis is contradicted. Entries followed by a question mark are borderline cases: for example, instances in which the signs in the given table were in the appropriate direction, but the size of the gamma coefficients was modest. The reader will also recall that we have concluded that some of our earlier hypotheses deal directly with portions of a larger concept of societal complexity. Where that is the case we have placed an asterisk below the name of the hypothesis. (Two asterisks denote hypotheses that are indirectly related to societal complexity.) Let us examine the final results in table 19.

The most general pattern to emerge is the series of associations with what we have called societal complexity. A simple society (see Marsh, 1967; Lenski, 1970) means in political terms a culture where the autonomous political unit is small (maybe just a few hundred people) and lacks a hierarchy of specialized offices and organizations. For most purposes lineage or community chieftains or simply heads of families exercise whatever leadership there is over the rest of the community. In terms of stratification a simple society means one in which there are few recognized social differences beside those of age and sex, and the ranking of individuals depends more upon personal qualities and skills than upon inherited wealth or status at birth. In economic terms this sort of society is one that relies mainly on hunting and gathering for subsistence, and in which there are no large

TABLE 19
The Fate of the Hypotheses

	1a	1b	1c	2a	2b	3	4	5	6	7	8	9	10a	10b	11	12	13	14a	14b	15	16
	Intensive Agriculture—	Animal Herding—	Hunting—	Warfare—	Warfare+	Male Solidarity—	Matrilineal Descent+ & Matrilocal Residence+	Extended Families—	Political Hierarchy—	Private Property—	Societal Complexity—	Classical Religion—	Envy—	Envy+	Female Shortage+ & Male Absence+	Women's Property+	Women's Work Organization+	Subsistence Role+	Subsistence Role—	Control Fruits+	Polyandry+
	(*)	(**)	(**)	(**)	(**)				(*)	(*)	(*)	(**)									
DVS 1: Property control	0	0	-?	0	0	0	+	0	+?	+?	+?	0	0	0	0	X	0	0	0	X	0
DVS 2: Kin power	0	0	+	0	0	0	0	0	0	0	+?	0	0	0	0	0	-?	0	0	0	X
DVS 3: Value of life	0	0	-?	-?	+?	0	+?	0	0	0	0	0	0	0	0	0	0	0	0	0	0
DVS 4: Value of labor	0	0	0	0	0	0	0	0	0	+	0	0	0	0	0	0	0	X	X	0	0
DVS 5: Domestic authority	+	+?	-	-	+	0	0	0	+	0	0	0	0	0	0	0	0	0	0	+?	0
DVS 6: Ritualized female solidarity	+	+	-	-?	+?	0	+?	0	+	0	0	+	0	0	0	0	X	0	0	0	0
DVS 7: Control of sex	+	0	0	0	0	0	+?	0	+?	+?	+	0	0	0	0	0	0	0	0	0	0
DVS 8: Ritualized fear	0	0	-?	0	0	0	+?	0	0	+?	+?	0	0	0	0	0	+?	0	0	+?	0
DVS 9: Joint participation	-?	-?	0	+	-	0	0	0	0	0	-?	0	0	0	0	0	0	0	0	0	0
DV 52: Informal influence	-	-?	+?	0	0	0	0	0	-	-?	-	-?	0	0	0	0	0	0	0	0	0

KEY: + = hypothesis supported; 0 = hypothesis not supported; — = hypothesis contradicted; ? = borderline cases; X = not applicable; (*) = independent variables directly related to societal complexity; (**) = independent variables indirectly related to societal complexity.

amounts of inheritable property. In terms of settlement patterns simple societies are ones in which people live in small groups that are often nomadic or seminomadic, and in terms of technology these societies tend to lack many of the tools used by people in other societies to exploit nature more efficiently.[12]

In such simple societies the division of authority within the home between husband and wife tends to be relatively equal, without a clear and automatic domination by the man. In such societies women tend not to have their social lives restricted to the home, but to engage in activities in solidary groups with other women in the community at large. At the same time there is a weak tendency for such societies to lack joint participation by men and women in community activities. The sexual and marital regulations in these societies do not restrict women much more than men, and perhaps this is the consequence of the relative absence of strict sexual regulations for anyone in many of these societies. Women are not noted for having a great deal of informal influence, and this seems to be associated with relative absence of positions and roles from which women in such societies are barred. At the same time women are not especially disadvantaged in their control over property; and this may reflect the fact that there is little valuable property in such societies for either sex to monopolize. In simple societies relying most heavily on hunting and warfare there is also somewhat more value placed on women's lives, but there is perhaps less of a tendency for women to share in kin-group leadership where hunting is important.

12. The grouping into simple and complex societies reflects a statistical tendency, rather than invariant rules. Any particular society may deviate from these generalizations in certain respects—e.g., a society may be simple in political terms, but rely on slash and burn agriculture rather than hunting and gathering; or a society that is nomadic may have a political structure with chiefs and subchiefs, and so forth.

155

Within our sample complex societies are those with more advanced tools and techniques, subsistence based primarily on intensive agriculture, large and stable settlements, large political units with a hierarchy of specialized offices, and stratification involving a complex set of classes or castes with differential control over private property and other resources. In these complex preindustrial societies we find the other side of the coins just described: Women tend to have less authority in the home, to lack joint rituals and solidarity with other women, to have more unequal restrictions placed on their sexual lives, and perhaps to have less control over property. In these societies women exercise their influence more informally and indirectly, often through their access to men who hold positions of formal authority. At the same time there is a weak tendency in such complex societies for men and women to participate together in work and community activities more than they do in simpler societies.

This pattern of associations with aspects of complexity accounts for the large majority of the findings in table 19. The few results that do not fit this one overall pattern have been noted previously: In societies with matrilineal descent and matrilocal postmarital residence, which we expect most often to be ones that are in the intermediate range of our complexity variables (see Aberle, 1961), women have more control over property and perhaps some other modest advantages. In societies without important private property the labor of women is more valuable than elsewhere. Women in cultures with classical religions also suffer some disadvantages that cannot be attributed solely to the general complexity of the cultures in which they live. Women who control the fruits of their own labor and the labor of others may enjoy some modest benefits relative to women in other societies. For the remainder of our study we will be mainly concerned with our primary finding concerning complexity, rather than with these few remaining consistent patterns.

On balance we have found that women in the most complex preindustrial societies suffer some disadvantages relative to men that women in simpler societies do not. These tables

156

fail to explain why it is that women are disadvantaged in such societies, and we must grapple with that issue here. What exactly are the reasons for these disadvantages? We can now exclude certain arguments that others have used to explain the "patriarchal" nature of peasant or agrarian societies. The important thing is clearly not that men do most of the plowing and agricultural work or control the inheritance of land, or lead large, extended families in such societies. Yet what is important? Our data help us to reject some possible explanations, but they do not direct us to the correct answers. Some insight can be drawn from recent theorizing by a number of anthropologists.

We find the works of Jack Goody (1969, 1973), supplemented by other work by Walter Goldschmidt and his colleagues (Goldschmidt and Kunkel, 1971; Michaelson and Goldschmidt, 1971) of greatest help in solving our puzzle. Goody is interested not in comparing simple hunting and gathering societies with agrarian states, but in comparing the horticultural and herding societies of precolonial sub-Saharan Africa with the agrarian societies of Eurasia. He presents a rather involved argument that bears on at least major portions of the relationships with societal complexity we have uncovered in this study. Sub-Saharan (or non-Islamic) Africa is an area in which the dowry is virtually absent, and where marriage finance consists generally of bride prices (or bridewealth, to use Goody's term). Eurasia, on the other hand, is characterized by dowries or by indirect dowries (the latter referring to a sum of goods and valuables provided by the groom's family that the bride brings back with her upon marriage, as she does a dowry). This difference in marriage finance is part of a larger complex of differences between the two regions, and these differences can also be seen in a worldwide sample (Goody, 1969).

Why the importance of dowry versus bridewealth? The dowry, Goody argues, tends to occur in general in peasant or agrarian societies where there is plow agriculture, intensive farming, high population density, and land shortage. In such societies there exists complex stratification based pri-

157

marily on differential ownership of scarce agricultural land (and to a lesser extent of draft animals). With important economic and status differences based upon land, parents (especially well-off ones) are concerned about preserving the status of their offspring: their sons through inheritance of land, and their daughters through dowries. Dowries are inherently variable, and families will try to accumulate large dowries in order to attract a desirable mate for their daughter (i.e., one with substantial inherited land or prospects of such an inheritance). Given the importance of status considerations in marriage, females can wreck their parents' calculations by independently forming romantic ties and becoming pregnant. Therefore in such societies parents will try to strictly control marriage choices and will emphasize female purity and virginity at marriage. (Male romantic and sexual involvements are less of a threat as long as they can be kept casual, and thus a premarital double standard emerges.)

The necessity of amassing a dowry will tend to delay the marriage of females, and they may be almost as old as, or even older than, their husbands. These societies also tend to be monogamous. The necessity of providing for sons through inheritance and daughters through dowries tends to disperse family property, and makes polygyny unlikely except among the very rich. The monogamous emphasis is heightened because women do not generally play a major role in agricultural labor, and there is often no spare land available to support another spouse and children (see Goldschmidt and Kunkel, 1971). This resulting monogamous tendency helps keep the age gap between husbands and wives small, since there are not large numbers of older males dipping into the pool of younger women to enlarge their number of wives. In these various tendencies of agrarian societies with dowries we can see an explanation for the association between complexity and the control over women's sexual lives (DVS 7) that we have detected.

Women in these complex societies receive a dowry as a form of inheritance in advance from their parents, but the

158

dowry generally consists of clothing, jewelry, furniture, and the like, but excludes productive property, particularly land. (We should note, however, that there are some exceptions to this pattern—agrarian societies in which daughters have regular inheritance rights to family property, including land. See Tambiah, 1973; Goldschmidt and Kunkel, 1971.) The woman's dowry and her husband's inheritance are pooled to form a conjugal fund or estate, which the husband generally manages. Thus women bring important valuables into the marriage, but their control over family property is severely limited, particularly regarding land. The establishment of the conjugal fund of property serves to emphasize the unity of the conjugal or immediate family group at the expense of any larger kin group or lineage (see Goldschmidt and Kunkel, 1971). Much of daily life is conducted in the family unit and managed by the husband or by his father, and a woman's participation in the larger community is generally as a member of this family unit, rather than as an individual woman joining together with other women. The relative unimportance of lineages or other corporate kin groupings also tends to focus the activities of men on the family farm or other enterprise, rather than in collective work or other activities with all other men in the community. The ways in which control over property and marriage finance are handled thus produce a strong emphasis on the individual family economy, and a de-emphasis on communitywide solidarities based upon sex. A high degree of joint husband-wife participation in the community is not so clearly a feature of complex peasant societies, since some of these have taboos on close contact between spouses in public and even rules confining married women to the immediate home environment, as in the well-known custom of purdah (see Michaelson and Goldschmidt, 1971). We can see emerging here in our discussion of agrarian societies with the dowry several other themes that our data in this chapter point to: particularly the limited rights in productive property women have (DVS 1) and the structured limitations on their solidarity with other women (DVS 6). The weaker relationship between complexity and joint social participation (DVS 9) is less clear; women in peasant societies may lack organized solidarity with other women, but in only some of them do they participate in work and community activities alongside of their husbands.

In bridewealth societies, particularly in precolonial Africa, Goody argues that things are quite different. These tend to be societies without intensive plow agriculture. Instead gardening based on hoes or digging sticks is combined with herding. Population densities are low, agriculture is often of the shifting variety, and individuals can generally gain access to as much land as they need. Such societies lack class differences based on differential landownership, although there may be politically based noble or chiefly lineages. In the absence of land shortage and class stratification, status concerns are not so important in marriage, and even marriages between members of noble lineages and slaves are recorded. Since there is less concern about differential access to land, parents have less reason to be concerned about controlling the marriage choices of their daughters. Bride prices tend to be relatively fixed and to circulate around the community, rather than downward from generation to generation, as with the dowry. Families less well off than their neighbors can still receive a bride price for marrying off a daughter and can use this to pay a bride price to get a mate for their son. Since there is not the difference between a "good match" and a "bad match" there is in a dowry system, there will be less emphasis on arranged marriage and less concern for virginity at marriage. (In fact Goody argues that in a patrilineal society parents may sometimes even encourage their daughters to have illegitimate children, since these children belong to a woman's natal kin group, while after marriage her children belong to her husband's group.) The necessity of accumulating a bride price delays the marriages of many males, while daughters will often be encouraged to marry early, in order to bring in bride prices that can be used to get brides for their brothers. A large age gap at marriage is also fostered by the emphasis on polygyny in most of these societies, which allows older men to accumulate extra wives. Taking extra wives makes some economic sense, since there is usually extra land available, women do an important share of the farm work, and the many sons and daughters produced will not disperse a finite amount of family property, as occurs in a dowry system. Thus in African bridewealth societies we see the opposite end of our scale for control over women's sexual and marital lives emerging (DVS 7).

In these less complex societies men and women do not establish a conjugal fund of property at marriage, and in many cases productive property is controlled by corporate kin groups rather than by the immediate family. Women are often excluded from rights to inheritance of land and cattle, but women can gain property in other ways. The financial activities of husbands and wives are characteristically distinct in these societies. Women engage in joint work activities with other women, and they may engage in marketing and other activities on their own account, without their husbands being responsible for their debts. In Goody's phrase, "From the financial point of view, husband and wife are not of one flesh" (Goody, 1973, p. 38). The property the woman does manage to acquire does not necessarily pass through her husband's hands or come under his management. She can often hold and accumulate valuable property and pass it on to her children separately from the husband (see also Friedl, 1975). In general the conjugal unit is not much emphasized in economic life, and many economic activities involve men from many households or women from many households. Women are not generally restricted to the home in these societies. We can see here the theme that in societies where the bridewealth operates, women more often engage in solidary activities with other women than is the case in more complex societies (DVS 6). The greater access women have to property (DVS 1) also comes through in a qualified way, although again our findings on joint social participation (DVS 9) are not as clear. Women clearly participate on an active basis in extrafamilial activities in most of these societies, but they do not particularly engage in such activities as couples with their husbands.

161

By following Goody's arguments we can begin to understand why it is that women in complex, agrarian societies suffer some of the disadvantages detected in our data. Basically the proposed causal connections are as follows:[13]

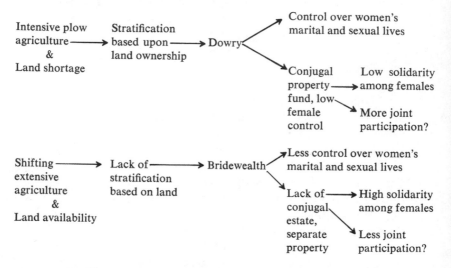

13. Given Goody's arguments, one puzzling question is why our scales for the power of women in kinship contexts (DVS 2), which includes measures of polygynous tendencies, and the value placed on the labor of women (DVS 4), which includes a dowry/bride price item, do not relate strongly to our measures of complexity. There are a number of possible explanations, including the fact that we have not differentiated in our codings between the true bride price and what Goody calls an indirect dowry, and the fact that both scales include other items unrelated to Goody's framework. However, we suspect the primary explanation is that Goody's argument focuses on the differences between horticultural and herding societies in Africa and agrarian societies of Eurasia, while our sample includes cultures of other types, particularly those based primarily on hunting and gathering, from around the world. Hunting and gathering societies tend to practice monogamy or limited polygyny rather than general polygyny, and in terms of marriage finance both substantial bride prices and dowries are generally absent. These features of the simplest cultures in our sample undermine any simple linear relationship between societal complexity and marriage finance or marriage type.

Goody's argument also helps us to explain the regional variation we found in table 18, and perhaps the religious effect shown in table 13. He points out that dowry and bride-wealth systems are not randomly distributed over the globe, with the dowry concentrated particularly in Eurasia (our circum-Mediterranean and east Eurasian regions, where we noted low scores on several scales). Yet even cultures lacking intensive agriculture may be affected by the family customs of their more powerful neighbors, as Goody shows in his discussion of the introduction of dowries with Islamic penetration into many parts of Africa.

We still lack a total explanation of our findings, however, since the low domestic authority and high informal influence of women in complex, agrarian societies do not flow directly out of Goody's framework. The finding for domestic authority may fit the argument indirectly. Goody speculates that in agrarian societies with the dowry, the control over women established before and during mate choice may continue afterward. Additionally in simpler societies the low emphasis on the conjugal bond and the prevalence of polygyny (with individual wives and their children often living separately from the husband) may give women more autonomy in managing domestic activities than they have in monogamous, solidary families where the dowry is common. However, complexity involves other things besides stratification and land shortage, in particular the proliferation of specialized extrafamilial roles, roles that tend to be monopolized by men. Just why it is that men dominate these roles is not clear from our study, although the universally greater burdens of child care borne by women may be a factor. Complex societies also have more hierarchical political systems, in which rule and domination are often legitimated by divine or natural right ideologies. These features give men more outlets and resources to use in dominating women, and more ideological support for the controls they place on their own wives and daughters. We are suggesting that women have less domestic authority and have to rely more on informal influence in

163

complex societies because of the specialized political and occupational hierarchies that such societies develop, hierarchies men tend to dominate. We conclude, then, that the disabilities of women in complex agrarian societies are due to a combination of factors: to the stratification and family property dynamics of intensive farming, the proliferation of extrafamilial roles dominated by men, and the increasingly hierarchical structure and ascriptive ideology of political institutions. Theorists of matriarchy and the decline of women are wrong when they talk of an earlier age ruled by women and a later universal mutiny of men, but they have a point when they note the relative disadvantage suffered by women in many peasant societies and classical kingdoms.[14] We can

14. We need to clarify how our argument in the preceding pages differs from the classical Marxist argument presented by Engels (1902). We stress here, as did Engels, that women in stratified agrarian societies suffer some disadvantages relative to women in simpler societies, and that some of these disadvantages are connected with differential control over private property, a growing stress on the individual family economic unit, and the emergence of centralized political institutions. Yet in a number of important areas we disagree with Engels, whose book is riddled with mistaken assumptions and factual errors.

Engels claims that in the period before the advent of stratified agrarian societies property was communally owned by matrilineal kin groups, that women shared equally in the subsistence work and ran the affairs of the extended matrilineal household, that "pairing marriages" existed that could easily be entered into and broken, that children were viewed as belonging to the entire kin group, with paternity of little concern, and that both men and women had much freedom to engage in sex acts with other partners. With the advent of the domestication of plants and animals and finally the technological advances that produced intensive agriculture, ownership of productive property (especially land) became increasingly important, as did the male role in farming, and private property monopolized by individual men emerged. Men used their control over private property and farming activities to subjugate women and to claim exclusive paternity over their children, as heirs to their property. In order to do this they subverted matriliny and replaced it with patrilineal descent, and they made their wives dependent upon them and their property, rather than upon the communal property of the kin group. This led to the mo-

164

now begin to understand more fully the bases of these disabilities.

However, it is extremely important to note that these disadvantages only apply to some of our scales. In tracing these relationships we can see that the pattern is most clear for domestic authority, ritualized female solidarity, control of sex, and informal influence and progressively weaker for our other dependent variable scales. In particular we have no hypothesized relationships, with complexity or anything else,

---

nogamous family emerging, in which the marital bond was stronger, while ties and obligations to wider kin were undermined. The wife increasingly became the domestic slave of the husband, rather than an active and equal participant in community life. The sexual double standard emerged at this time, as men continued to be able to have outside affairs while their wives were forbidden to do so. For purposes of comparison with Goody's scheme, we can diagram the causal links described by Engels as follows:

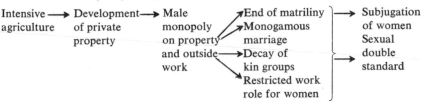

We disagree with Engels's formulation on at least the following grounds:

a) Private property in the means of production exists more widely in societies simpler than this scheme allows; it is not simply the product of advanced agriculture or the influence of foreign colonialists. Horticultural and even hunting and gathering societies in our sample have mixtures of private property and broader ownership of important forms of productive property.

b) As we have noted earlier, there is no evidence for a general matrilineal stage in human evolution. However, it is true that where matriliny exists, intensive agriculture tends to undermine it.

c) Private property does not seem to be the crucial variable in producing most of the changes in the role of women, as we saw in testing hypothesis 7. Relationships with other aspects of societal complexity are generally stronger. Moreover, women's exclusion from control over property and valued goods does not seem a crucial factor

165

strongly confirmed for our scale of ritualized fear of women by men. Our scale of the relative contribution of women to subsistence has a strong relationship only with our scale for the presence or absence of private property (with female contributions more important where such property is absent), and our scale of the power of women in kinship realms shows only one clear relationship, already mentioned, with the importance of hunting. What factors are related to the fact that women do most of the subsistence work in one society and little of the work in another? What factors contribute to tendencies for men to be able to take many wives in some societies and not in others? Or for men to have grave fears of sexual contamination from women in some societies but not in others? In this study we have not only found that the status of women is not the unitary phenomenon we supposed it to be, but that only some components of our original conception can be confidently associated with variations in the set of independent variables we have used. We have come a long way in our understanding of the lot of women, but important questions remain unanswered.

---

in her downfall, as we saw in testing hypotheses 12 and 15. Nor does the relative contribution of men and women to subsistence have a key effect, as we saw in testing hypotheses 14a and 14b. In other words, the key links in the logical argument presented by Engels are not supported by our evidence. The transition to stratified, agrarian societies is an important one, but Goody's explanation of the causal connections is closer to the truth than Engels's.

d) In general Engels exaggerates the difference between the lot of women in stratified, agrarian societies and in simpler societies, as in his famous statement, "The overthrow of mother right [as a result of the advent of private property] was the *world historical defeat of the female sex*. The man took command in the home also; the woman was degraded and reduced to servitude; she became the slave of the husband and a mere instrument for the production of children" (Engels, 1902, pp. 120-121, emphasis in original). The differences seem to us both more subtle and, as we note above, more limited.

166

CHAPTER VII

Conclusions

WE set out to learn how the status of women relative to men varies cross-culturally and why, and along the way we found ourselves led from this simple question into ever more complicated problems. Now we must stand back and see what we have learned, and how much our findings modify previously accepted theories. The challenges our findings represent for some established ideas are substantial.

Many writings by both partisans and skeptics of the women's liberation movement depict existing and previous societies as universally emphasizing male dominance over women. For the feminists this universal male dominance is seen as the result of factors that can and will change (such as the past importance of male strength in subsistence activities), while the skeptics are most apt to search for biological and genetic arguments for why this dominance will remain inevitable in future societies. Our findings lead us to qualify the statements and assumptions coming from both sides. We do not find a pattern of universal male dominance, but much variation from culture to culture in virtually all aspects of the position of women relative to men. Our findings do lead us to doubt that there are any cultures in which women are totally dominant over men, since few of our individual variables in chapter IV are skewed strongly in favor of women. Yet from this it does not follow that in all societies men are absolutely dominant over women. Rather, there is substantial variation from societies with very general male dominance to other societies in which broad equality and even some specific types of female dominance over men exist. Women seem never to fully dominate men in all of social life, but the degree of male dominance ranges from total to minimal.

The whole notion of assuming universal male dominance and then looking for universal explanations for that dubious assumption seems to us an unproductive enterprise. It will be more useful to examine the relative share of women in political power and how this varies cross-culturally than to simply stop with the assertion that men tend to monopolize political positions in every society. Also, instead of simply stating that boys everywhere tend to be socialized to be aggressive and girls to be passive, we should examine how cultures differ in stressing or de-emphasizing such differences.

Once we drop the focus on universals and accept the reality of cross-cultural variation, we are led to take issue with another large category of misleading assumptions. A few writers, such as Lowie, start by assuming that different aspects of the rights, powers, and roles of women relative to men are not related, unless proved otherwise. However, the opposite assumption is much more common: that different aspects of the status and position of women in social life naturally vary together. Indeed, it does make things much simpler if we can assume that there is such a thing as *the* status of women, and that all of its aspects are closely related in the real world. We commonly find writers who make this assumption talking about women's work roles at one moment and switching to discuss the differential socialization of the sexes or relative sexual restrictions on women the next. If there were such a coherent phenomenon as the status of women, then talking about any aspect of it would be as good as talking about any other (since they would all tend to vary closely together). Moreover, if such a general status of women complex existed, by explaining why any particular aspect of it, such as relative sexual restrictions, varied from one culture to another, we would have explained why the general complex as a whole varied.

However, reality is not so simple. In chapter IV we discovered that our variables had divergent cross-cultural dis-

168

tributions. Some, such as items for political leadership, are highly skewed in favor of men; others, such as property inheritance or access to roles as shamans, are more moderately skewed toward men; still others, such as the elaborateness of funerals or final authority over infants, show little or no male bias cross-culturally, or even show a bias in favor of women. In chapter V we discovered that, with limited exceptions, these different indicators of the relative place of women in social life are not associated with each other. Knowing how much access to political power women have in a given society will not allow us to predict with any confidence how free of restrictions their sexual lives will be, or how much of the work of the society women will perform. Since these different indicators vary pretty much independently, we were led to the conclusion that there is no such thing as *the* status of women. Different aspects of this supposedly unitary concept are not substitutable for one another, and being able to explain the variation in one aspect will not help you to explain the variation in others.

Once these complexities are accepted we were further led to conclude that some things that have been assumed in the existing literature to have status implications for women may not. For example, there now seem to be no grounds for assuming that the relative subsistence contribution of women has any general status implications. It appears that in some societies where women do most of the productive work they have certain kinds of high status, while in others where women are similarly important economically they are systematically discriminated against in many ways. (We emphasize this finding because in many studies it is assumed obvious, following Engels's argument, that work outside the home tends to give women higher overall status. In fact, in one recent study—see Sanday, 1973—a slight *negative* association was found between the subsistence contribution of women and certain status indicators. The author, undaunted by this finding, proceeded to argue that this showed that women's productive labor was a necessary, but not sufficient,

169

condition for high status. Yet strong convictions cannot explain away negative results.) We have concluded that some of our scales, such as the relative control women have over property, do have status implications, but only because it seems inherently preferable to have more property rather than less and not because by controlling more property women also gain political rights, sexual freedoms, and so forth.

These conclusions pose a series of cautions for future researchers and writers on the role of women: One can no longer assume that there is such a thing as *the* status of women cross-culturally. Nor can one assume that a favorable position for women in any particular area of social life will be related to favorable positions in other areas. Nor can one search for *the best* indicator of the status of women, or for *the key* variable that affects the status of women. Instead one now has to start with a very different assumption: that there is no coherent concept of the status of women that can be identified cross-culturally, and that when we think we are looking at aspects or indicators of the status of women we are dealing with essentially unrelated things. A finding of a favorable or unfavorable situation for women in regard to divorce or property rights will not tell you much beyond just that: how women fare in terms of access to divorce or control over property. A feature of social structure that seems to explain part of the cross-cultural variation in women's subsistence contribution or domestic authority can only explain those things, and cannot explain how women's solidary organizations or informal influence vary. In other words, each aspect of the status, roles, and relationship of women relative to men must be examined and explained separately, unless future research shows a cross-cultural reality that is very different from the patterns we have discovered.

Since we were not able to locate any general status of women syndrome empirically, we were left with several more or less independent scales measuring aspects of the status, roles, and relationship of the sexes. In chapter VI we systematically investigated why some societies in our sample have

170

higher scores on these separate measures than others, and our method was to test a series of hypotheses. Once again our results did not fit the assumptions of much current writing about the position of women. Warfare and hunting do not seem to be associated with male domination, nor does the relative share of subsistence work done by women make much difference in any of our measures. In general the fact that important activities in a society require male strength does not by itself lead to the subordination of women. Frequent male absence does not seem to elevate the status of women cross-culturally, nor do societies with a fair amount of sex-role insecurity and sexual envy seem to have either higher or lower scores on our scales. Institutionalized exclusively male groups do not seem to be associated with low status for women, nor do exclusively female work groups seem to be associated with high status. Also, the fact that a man rather than a woman studies a particular culture does not seem to lead to a systematic male bias in the picture given of the position of women in that society. These are only some of the more significant of our *negative* findings.

When the rejected hypotheses were cleared away, a few of our original hypotheses did yield positive results. The cross-cultural variation in certain aspects of the relative status, roles, and relationship of the sexes seems at least partly understandable. Matrilineal descent and matrilocal residence are associated with modest benefits for women in certain areas (particularly in property rights), and the existence of private property is associated with some forms of male bias (particularly the low value placed on the labor of women). However, it should be noted that neither of these factors has the sweeping consequences for women that some of the earlier literature supposed. There is no evidence that either a shift to patrilineal descent and patrilocal residence or the emergence of private property rights is *the* crucial step in some postulated decline of women. We also discovered, as we have already noted, that reliance on hunting and frequent warfare in a society are associated with certain limited kinds of bene-

171

fits for women (in domestic authority and independent female solidarity).

The most consistent pattern to emerge in chapter VI, however, was the series of associations with measures of societal complexity, a concept that, as we mentioned at the outset of this study, serves as our "proxy" in dealing with questions of social evolution. We don't have a true evolutionary sequence in our sample, since our data on each culture all refer to one point in time. Yet through a series of variables we can compare cultures that have features that emerged early in the scale of human evolution (pottery making, nomadic bands) with cultures having features that emerged relatively late (the plow, settled towns and cities). It is this sort of comparison that shows the strongest and most consistent results. In the more complex cultures, women tend to have less domestic authority, less independent solidarity with other women, more unequal sexual restrictions, and perhaps receive more ritualized fear from men and have fewer property rights, than is the case in the simpler cultures. At the same time women in these more complex cultures tend to have more informal influence and perhaps somewhat more joint participation with males. We have argued that these differences are associated in part with the nature of intensive farming and the differentiated class structure of our complex societies, features that place a premium on controlling women's sexual and marital lives and that also produce conjugal property estates and family farms, which set the family apart from wider solidarities, including those with other women. We think another part of this pattern may be due to the presence of many specialized roles outside the family and complex political hierarchies legitimated by ascriptive ideologies. These features may limit the domestic authority of women and require them to exert their influence in the wider society informally, through their menfolk.

On balance, and even with allowance for the fact that not all of our scales have clear status implications, the lot of women would seem to be somewhat better in the simpler societies in our sample than in the more complex ones. The problems of women in the more complex societies are specific and not general, but the relative disadvantages suffered by women in these societies in certain areas of social life are repeatedly borne out in our data. Yet what about the most complex societies that exist, the societies we live in today? Can our findings be generalized to industrialized nation-states, and if so how? Do our findings tell us anything about the prospects for women's liberation movements and the strategies they should employ? These are difficult questions to deal with, and our answers can only be tentative.

As explained in chapter II, this is a cross-cultural survey. Its units are local settlements and ethnic subgroups that are relatively homogeneous culturally, rather than nation-states and multiethnic societies. Furthermore, with limited exceptions (e.g., a rural Japanese village in 1950), the cultures in our sample are preindustrial, and many of them are preliterate as well. The variables we used in comparing such cultures (dealing with such things as shamans and menstrual taboos) are in some cases of limited interest in dealing with industrialized nation-states, while other variables (relative wage rates, educational participation rates) that our study does not include become much more important. Given these systematic differences, no automatic generalization of our findings to the world of modern nation-states is possible. However, we can at least speculate about what we might find if we conducted a cross-national rather than a cross-cultural survey.

We found cross-culturally that there was much variation in the way different measures of the role of women relative to men are distributed. We would expect to find such a pattern in a cross-national survey as well. We know that national political leadership posts are heavily monopolized by men in all societies (but with some variation in degree), while there is less male bias in things such as property ownership and labor force participation. In some societies access to education is heavily biased in favor of males, while in others it is

173

not, but in most contemporary societies ceremonies for child-birth or death tend to be similarly elaborate for males and females. We would expect our warning about the need to specify what aspect of the role of women relative to men you are talking about when making comparisons to be just as applicable in modern nations as in preliterate cultures.

We also found that statistical associations among various aspects of the role and status of women were very weak, leading us to conclude that most aspects vary independently of each other. It is less clear whether we should expect this same pattern to emerge if we conducted a cross-national survey, but we see no reason why it would not. In other words, it is not clear that there is anything about the nature of large nation-states that would lead such national indicators of the role and status of women as we could construct to cohere into a single identifiable status of women syndrome, if they do not do so in a sample of preindustrial cultures. Some common observations support this line of argument. It has frequently been observed that in American society women have received certain kinds of polite and chivalrous treatment from men, while their occupational opportunities have been quite limited. To take another example, we have not seen it argued that Swiss women, deprived of the vote long after women's suffrage had swept the world, are more systematically disadvantaged relative to men in the rest of social life than are women in other societies. A few scholarly studies have commented on the failure of different aspects of the role of women to change together in modern times. Joan Scott and Louise Tilly (1975) note that women's labor force participation changed little from the mid-nineteenth to the early twentieth centuries in England, France, and Italy, while during this period marked changes in women's property and political rights took place. Michael Sacks (1974) has shown that, while the labor force participation of women shot up markedly between the 1920s and 1960s in the Soviet Union, time budget studies in the two periods show that there was no change at all in the relative time husbands

174

and wives spent on domestic chores (with women, of course, still saddled with most of this burden). Our own research dealing with China since 1949 (Parish and Whyte, 1978) indicates that rural women receive more education, work more outside the home, and contribute more to family income than they used to, but that they still have little formal voice in local village leadership, do the great bulk of the domestic work, have not gained significantly in property rights or rights to their children in the event of divorce, and so forth. The complexities we have found in the present study of pre-industrial cultures seem to be mirrored in the life of women in large nation-states.

These observations do not, of course, prove the case, and the results of our own cross-cultural survey have repeatedly shown us the dangers of generalizing from such ad hoc examples. It would be necessary to carry out a cross-national survey paralleling this study to be certain one way or the other. It is conceivable that such a study could be carried out, although the sparseness of national data on a number of topics would constitute a problem (see, for example, Ferriss, 1971). A sample of societies could be drawn, and then a combination of census, journalistic, legal, questionnaire, and other kinds of data used to construct a wide variety of indicators: relative educational attendance of men and women, relative wage rates, marriage ages, involvement in the labor force, property rights, and so forth. We see no a priori reason why the level of statistical associations among such measures should be any greater than that found among the quite different set of indicators used in our study.

From the lack of associations among our variables cross-culturally, we concluded that there is no crucial aspect of the status or role of women such that an improvement there will have a favorable impact on many other aspects as well. Assuming that a similar pattern would emerge in a cross-national study, it would provide some understanding of the uneven progress of feminism in the West, and in particular of the unspectacular results of success in the women's suf-

175

frage drive. It can be argued that getting the vote had very little impact on women's roles in other areas of social life; getting the vote meant primarily getting the vote, and not much more. It did not have the far-reaching consequences that either advocates or opponents of the suffrage movement thought it would. To cite another example, it can be argued that the shift from formal education being primarily a male prerogative to universal education for both sexes has not radically altered the economic or domestic roles of women. Similarly, we would expect that the current drive in many societies to open up more job opportunities for women and to get them out of the house and into the offices and factories would not result in dramatic improvements in the way husbands treat wives or in the percentage of women holding high political office.

This lack of association between different measures of the role and status of women relative to men still constitutes something of a puzzle. Why aren't women's property rights and women's domestic authority more closely related? Or women's economic contribution and their sexual rights? In the study of stratification we ordinarily expect indicators of status at the individual level to be positively, although not perfectly, associated with one another. Thus a person with high occupational prestige will tend to have had more education that most, to receive more income, and to have higher community status and political influence. There is also a much-debated theme in the stratification literature that says when an individual has discordant rankings on different status scales—for example, when he has high income but low education, or high income but low community standing— he may be led by this "status inconsistency" (see Lenski, 1954; Jackson, 1962) to have psychological anxieties or to join political or social movements designed to redress the balance or to relieve the anxieties. On the group level we also tend to think that aspects of status will have consequences for each other, so that a formerly downtrodden group, whether it be blacks, proletarians, or Irish immigrants, will use gains

176

in one area of social life (e.g., political power or economic strength) to strive for and achieve gains in other areas. This tendency fits the "resource theory" of social stratification (see Coleman, 1971; Blood and Wolfe, 1960). This theory asserts that stratification is essentially a battle for access to, or control over, strategic resources, in which groups will use the resources they have in the struggle to gain others. Thus for groups, as for individuals, we expect status inconsistencies to lead to strains and to actions designed to right the balance. Yet our cross-cultural findings lead us to suppose that when the group we are talking about is women, this doesn't hold true. Just why that should be so is the puzzle.

Partly this lack of association in our sample may be attributable to the cultural peculiarities and varied historical development of our cultures. One culture may explain its male preference in inheritance rights as stemming from a past instruction laid down by the gods, while another culture may consider a similar male bias the natural consequence of their hunting way of life. A social change that produces a shift in inheritance patterns in one culture may have no effect in another culture, due to the presence in the latter of some distinctive feature that counteracts the effect on property rights of the change in question. Even social structural factors that affect property rights in many societies may have little effect on, say, the relative sexual restrictions on men and women, which have their origins in quite different factors. In other words the great variety of cultural and social structural combinations around the world, and the complexities of the interactions and influences among them tend to make it unlikely that any two variables, such as property rights and sexual restrictions, will have the same relationship and will be seen by men and women as having the same implications, in different cultures in our sample. However, this is a general feature of cross-cultural studies. Such studies tend to produce weaker statistical associations among variables than do studies comparing cultures and societies that are quite similar. Yet cross-cultural studies do not all result in associations that are

177

close to zero, and in our study some of our associations (such as those between aspects of societal complexity and some of our women's scales) are quite respectable. If we want to explain why our associations among different indicators of the role and status of women are not simply modest, but in most cases negligible, it seems that we need to look for other reasons besides simply the diversity and peculiarity of world cultures.

One such reason may be proposed. In recent polemics the phrases "woman as nigger" and "woman as proletarian" have been used, but the symbolism obscures the fact that women do not react and interact in social life the way other oppressed groups have, and the most obvious reason seems to be that the institution of the family makes women fundamentally different from a class or a status group. This difference has been stated most eloquently by Simone de Beauvoir (1949, pp. 19-20):

> The proletarians have accomplished the revolution in Russia, the Negroes in Haiti, the Indo-Chinese are battling for it in Indo-China, but the women's effort has never been anything more than a symbolic agitation. . . . The reason for this is that women lack concrete means for organizing themselves into a unit which can stand face to face with the correlative unit. They have no past, no history, no religion of their own; and they have no such solidarity of work and interest as that of the proletariat. . . . They live dispersed among the males, attached through residence, housework, economic condition and social standing to certain men—fathers or husbands—more firmly than they are to other women. . . . The proletariat can propose to massacre the ruling class, and a sufficiently fanatical Jew or Negro might dream of getting sole possession of the atomic bomb and making humanity wholly Jewish or black; but women cannot even dream of exterminating the males. The bond that unites her to her oppressors is not comparable to any other. The division of sexes is a bio-

logical fact, not an event in human history. . . . The couple is a fundamental unity with its two halves riveted together, and the cleavage of society along the line of sex is impossible. Here is to be found the basic trait of woman: she is the other in a totality of which the two components are necessary to one another.

Added to this "unity with the oppressor" women experience another universal: The fact that women everywhere have the primary burden of early child care. There may be other factors as well, perhaps biological or hormonal differences, but it is clear that there are powerful factors existing in all societies that lead women (and men) to see their positions in society as differential roles without the kind of status implications that apply to occupational or ethnic groups. The particular division of roles between men and women is quite varied cross-culturally: In some cultures women are burdened with most of the food production and also have an active role in community decision making; in others women are expected to confine their activities to the home and hearth, and men hold sway in community affairs. Neither situation seems to lead to the women sensing their distinction from men in a true status group or class sense (i.e., developing "class consciousness"), and using their existing powers and resources to gain more favorable positions in other spheres of social life.

Has this situation perhaps changed with the rise of the women's liberation movement, with its consciousness-raising groups and political organizing? Have these new forces produced a fundamental change in the thinking of women, such that they will no longer de-emphasize the status implications of sex-role differentiation and will more actively use their existing powers to wrest gains from men? Again we cannot be certain without conducting a study of those modern industrial societies in which the women's liberation movement is a force. Yet the analysis presented here leads us to be cautiously skeptical. We have concluded that the lack of

179

association between different aspects of the role and status of women relative to men is due largely to the fact that women as a group are fundamentally different from status groups and classes. The reason for this difference stems from the interdependence of women and men and the obligations women have toward young children within the family, factors which are lacking for blacks, proletarians, and other low-status groups. In spite of certain discontents with marital fulfillment in modern societies, the women's liberation movement has not produced any significant change in the importance of the family as an institution in these societies, nor does it seem likely to. Thus the sources of the "special" features of women in social stratification do not seem to have been affected by recent trends.

If this reasoning is correct, then the prospects for improvement in the lot of women in modern societies seem to be as follows: Change will continue to be a complex and difficult thing. There are no magic keys such that one particular breakthrough for women in legal rights, job participation, or sexual liberation will bring about general equality in all of social life. The obstacles to equality in various spheres will continue to be different and will have to be attacked separately. Perhaps some goals—for example, equal access for women to national leadership posts—will continue to remain unobtainable. Yet these facts can be looked at more positively. Our analysis suggests that there is no inevitable obstacle to change in the role of women; no inherent or biological barrier that must prevent women from attaining equality in any area of social life. Even if equality in political leadership proves unobtainable (and our data do not prove that it will be), this does not mean that women cannot achieve more sexual equality or domestic authority. Aspects of the relationship of women to men are subject to change, but they will change in different ways and by overcoming different obstacles. In some ways this complexity is an unsatisfying fact, particularly for those who are intent on find-

180

ing the magic key to unlock all of the mysteries of social life, but our study suggests that reality holds no such magic keys.

Can we expect change in modern societies to be beneficial for women, i.e., to produce greater equality of the sexes? Is it not just as likely, or perhaps more likely, that the trend will be toward greater sexual inequality in the long run? We found in chapter VI that women in more complex societies in our sample tend to suffer certain kinds of disadvantages in comparison with women in simpler societies. Can we not expect this to be even more true in societies more complex than those in our sample, in our own and in future societies? In this case we can say no, we don't expect the trends uncovered in our sample to apply to modern industrial (and postindustrial) societies. Here there is some existing research to rely on, particularly the cross-national information presented by Goode (1963). That study found evidence in six major nations or regions of the world for modernization to benefit women. The trend as we move from agrarian to industrial societies seems to be one of decreasing, rather than increasing, inequality between the sexes in certain respects: legal rights, sexual restrictions, access to divorce, and so forth. It looks, therefore, as if the evolutionary trend, which within our sample appears to be linear, is actually curvilinear, with women in complex industrial societies regaining some of the equality that is lost in the transition from simple hunting and gathering societies to settled agrarian empires.

Why should this be the case? Goode's study provides some clues, but he frankly admits that the sorts of primary variables he is dealing with (the impact of industrialization and urbanization) are not sufficient to explain many of the kinds of increasing equality of women that he noted in societies around the world. We may achieve some greater understanding if we refer back to our analysis of the apparently linear evolutionary patterns in chapter VI. There we concluded that there were at least three separate aspects of increasing complexity that led women in agrarian kingdoms to

181

CONCLUSIONS

suffer some disadvantages relative to their sisters in nomadic hunting and gathering societies. One is the fact that
part of the definition of complexity is the differentiation
of new social roles outside of the family context, and the
greater outlet for male domination that these new roles supply. Another factor is that increasing political hierarchy and
autocratic ideologies seem to be associated with similar tendencies in much of the rest of social life, including the relationship between husbands and wives. Finally, complexity
also means the increasing importance of intensive agriculture, which is associated with a greater need to control the
family farm property and labor force, which also means
more control over wives and daughters.

Taking these three aspects of societal complexity, we can
see that at least two of them are checked or reversed when
agrarian societies become industrialized. Differentiation of
new roles and new opportunities for status achievement
is the aspect that is not reversed and in fact tends to ac-
celerate with modernization. However, autocratic kingdoms
give way to other political forms, many of which have
an egalitarian emphasis. Even though political hierarchies
may not be significantly compressed, new forms of participatory politics emerge, and traditional notions that certain
groups or individuals are destined by nature to rule over
others give way to expansion of citizenship rights and egalitarian justifications for the existing concentrations of power
(e.g., of the people, by the people, and for the people).[1] This
participatory and egalitarian ethos may have its "halo effect"

1. Several recent studies (see Holter, 1970; Blake, 1974) stress this
change, using a different terminology. In modern industrial societies
an emphasis on achievement and universalism increasingly replaces
one on ascription and particularism. As the legitimacy of ascription as
a principle for organizing society and rewarding positions is undermined, all kinds of inequalities that are based on ascriptive principles,
including sexual inequality, are also undermined. In terms of political
institutions it is not so much increasing equality of power that is important, but increasing equality of rights to compete for and hold
political offices and participate in political affairs in other ways.

182

back on relations between the sexes, undermining male domination of women. Finally, industrialization means the declining importance of agriculture in the economy, and a similar decline in the family as a basis for economic production. As new occupations emerge and increasingly set the pattern for modern life the traditional economic motivations for control of the destinies and sex lives of family members become less important. As concern for marriage alliances, dowries, and maintaining the family labor force become increasingly irrelevant, some of the disadvantages suffered by women in peasant societies can and do diminish.

What we are saying is that some of the social structural factors that produced the specific kinds of barriers to sexual equality in complex agrarian societies (in comparison with simpler societies) are reversed when we move further into even more complex industrial societies. The reversal of the trend toward inequality between the sexes that Goode documented in industrializing and industrialized societies seems to make sense, in terms of the analysis we have made of our own cross-cultural data.

Our findings from preindustrial cultures are not automatically applicable to modern nation-states. Yet what we have learned in this study about the vague and complex phenomena that revolve around the relative roles, status, and relationships of men and women has led us to some tentative statements and predictions. Many explanations of the position of women in social life that have gained great currency in public discussions seem misleading or simply wrong. Different aspects of what we originally supposed was a unitary phenomenon called "the status of women" turn out to be little related to each other, and to respond to different social forces and changes. There is no key barrier to the equality of women such that, if it falls, all other barriers will fall as well. Moreover, women because of their distinctive interdependence with men do not, and are not likely to, relate to status concerns in the same fashion as other oppressed groups. Each existing form of inequality between the

183

sexes must be attacked separately, using different tactics, and some may prove much harder to overcome than others. Yet the evolutionary tendencies present in modern industrial societies seem to present favorable opportunities for at least certain kinds of increasing equality between the sexes. Whether total equality in any real sense is possible remains uncertain, but we can expect women to continue to regain some of the ground they lost relative to men when humans first abandoned a simple hunting and gathering way of life thousands of years ago.

APPENDIX 1

Methodology

THIS study uses an alternate-case subsample of the Standard Cross-Cultural Sample devised by Murdock and White (1969). As explained by Murdock and White, the order in which their sample is arranged is determined by relative distance and cultural similarity among cultures. Thus cutting out every other culture leaves us with a sample in which the relative similarity and historical connections among adjacent cultures in our sample are proportionately reduced. Which half of the sample was used was determined by a simple flip of the coin, and the odd-numbered cultures won. (For a listing of the sample, see appendix 2.) The use of this standard sample promotes the possibility of comparisons with the work of other scholars using the same sample, including the codings for a number of areas of social life presented in recent editions of the journal *Ethnology*. In this study, however, we have conducted all of our own codings independently with the exception of the regional code (CV 11), which is taken from the Murdock and White article, and no systematic comparisons with other existing codings using this sample are undertaken in this volume.

As mentioned briefly in chapter II, this standard cross-cultural sample has a number of advantages over many previous samples used in this type of research. Murdock and his associates reviewed the information on over 1,250 known cultures in an effort to group them into clusters of similar cultures in order to form the basis for a sample covering the known range of world cultural diversity without duplication. This process resulted in the formulation of World Sampling Provinces (Murdock, 1968), which formed the basis for drawing the sample. Murdock and his associates

made an effort to include complex cultures as well as the
"primitive" and "preliterate" societies that are the staple of
cross-cultural research, and the sources on some of these are
the work of historians and archaeologists rather than anthropologists. Adequacy of coverage was a general criterion in
selection of the cultures, in order to assure a sample that
would be useful for research on a wide range of topics. (Many
earlier researchers used the less satisfactory procedure of
selecting a sample partly according to what sources were
available on the particular topic they were investigating.)
Murdock and White also made an effort to include cultures
described in languages other than English in order to avoid
the kinds of selective bias that arise when only cultures described by English-speaking researchers are used. In the
process they did not restrict their search to the cultures
covered in the Human Relations Area Files, and as a result
only 62 out of our 93 cultures were covered at least partially by the HRAF sources. Foreign language sources included in the HRAF are translated into English, but to handle
such sources in the rest of our sample we had to have at
least two coders able to read French, German, Spanish, and
Russian with ease.

The Murdock and White sample is also designed to minimize problems of diversity of sources and referents for particular cultures by specifying a precise time (the "anthropological present") and a particular local community or group
to be focused on in the coding. In general they tried to choose
the earliest period for which good descriptions of a particular
culture were available. In a number of cases we found that
the authorities and sources indicated by Murdock and White
did not satisfy their aims too well. We sometimes had trouble
finding the local community in the sources (e.g., the
Thonga) or in telling which of the source materials referred
to the specified time (e.g., the Creek). Problems in locating
sources led us in two cases, the Marquesans and the Cambodians, to substitute a more recent time period for the one

specified by Murdock and White, and in many cases we used somewhat different or additional sources. Interested scholars can obtain a complete list of the sources used by writing to the author.

Work on the project began, with the assistance of Kristin Moore, by formulating a preliminary coding form of items dealing with the status of women, and variables we thought might have some association with high or low status. A limited pretest of this preliminary form was then carried out using four graduate student coders, who coded selected even-numbered cultures from the Standard Cross-Cultural Sample. The primary purpose of the pretest was to clear up ambiguities in the wording of coding categories, and to eliminate items for which little information could be found. As indicated in chapters III and IV, the latter purpose was not fully served, since the final coding form contained a number of items for which little information could be found. For example, we planned to include a large number of items on differential childbearing of boys and girls from Barry, Bacon, and Child (1957). Yet we found such information so scarce that, as a result of the pretest, we reduced these codes to only two items, DV 43 and DV 44. In general in formulating our coding form we relied heavily on the kinds of items that had been used in earlier cross-cultural work by Murdock, Young, and others, in hopes of achieving some kinds of comparability with previous studies.

The actual coding began in September 1971 and continued for 20 months. Limited financial resources, and the need to suspend work at one point while new fund applications were pending, caused the work to drag out, and coders to come and go, far more than was anticipated or desired. In retrospect it would have been better to seek more funds at the outset and then hire assistants to work half- or even full-time in order to speed up the coding process. (All of our research assistant-coders worked part-time, generally around 10 hours a week, and in total 17 individuals took

187

part in the coding.) Not having conducted this sort of research before, the author did not realize the amount of time that the laborious coding would entail.

Those taking part in the coding, in addition to the author, were predominantly graduate students in either sociology or anthropology at the University of Michigan. After being hired they were all made aware of the general purpose of the study and given instructions in the use of the coding form. With the exception of the author, they were not aware of the specific hypotheses being investigated. Two coders read all of the assigned source materials on each culture. Each was instructed to make his or her codings based upon the material in the full source materials, rather than using the kinds of shortcuts available in the Human Relations Area Files. Source materials in the HRAF categorized files are found there both in their original monograph or article form (in translation as well as in the original foreign language version), and also in the form of separate pages that are filed under numbers indicating different cultural traits. For instance, there is a category 562, which is supposed to include any pages with information about the status of women. Even though there are ample cross-references within this filing system, there still is room for error and omission, and we opted to code cultures contained in the HRAF using the original sources, rather than this system of pages filed by categories.

The cover of each coding sheet contained detailed coding guidelines. The procedure was for each coder to flip back and forth through the indexed coding form, filling in items and making notes and page references in the margins as he or she went along. Coders were instructed not to "squeeze" information into codes if the information was ambiguous, and to make explanatory notes whenever they felt some doubt about a coding decision. Where information was ambiguous or lacking, or when two sources gave conflicting information, the coders were instructed to make liberal use of the "no information, ambiguous" codes accompanying each item.

188

When the item called for a "present" or "absent" judgment, coders were instructed to code "absent" if there was much discussion of the available topic but no mention of the specific practice, but to code "ambiguous" if there was no mention of the practice and little information on the general topic area.

When the first coder finished using the assigned sources he or she would check for gaps in the coding sheet. When large parts of the form remained empty this coder was instructed to look for additional sources, preferably on the same group and for the same year, using available ethnographic bibliographies (see O'Leary, 1970). When such additional sources were used the coder was instructed to fill the gaps only when he or she could be reasonably sure, in the case of deviation of the new sources from the time and place specified in our sample, that the new information would also apply to the originally specified time and group. If there was some evidence of change over time or local variation on a cultural trait, they were told not to base a coding on this new information. The second coder was then assigned these additional sources as well as those initially assigned, with similar directions. Coders were not informed in advance of who was doing the other coding on the same culture, and consulting of the other person's coding form was not allowed.

While making primary codings on our independent and dependent variables, coders were also making secondary codings. Secondary code A served to indicate that a trait coded had not been that way at an earlier time period. Code B indicated that the trait in question had changed since the anthropological present. Code C stood for a situation in which a distinct portion of the local community (e.g., elites, minorities) followed a custom different from that coded for the bulk of the local population. Code D was to be used where other communities within the same ethnic or tribal unit were said to have customs different from the community being coded. While these secondary codings may be useful in further analysis of our data we have not used them in this study. Coders also recorded at the beginning of the

189

form information about the source materials used and the characteristics of the authorities. These codings form the basis for our quality control checks (see chapter II), and they are listed in appendix 3.

After a culture had been coded twice, the next step was cross-checking for reliability. The coders assembled their coding forms and the sources at hand, and checked their codings against each other one at a time. Where codings agreed no problems arose. When there was a disagreement the coders inspected their marginal notes and/or the sources themselves in an effort to resolve the conflict. Where one of the coders had missed or misinterpreted the relevant information it was fairly easy for both to agree on the correct coding. However, they were instructed not to force a false resolution of a real conflict of interpretations, but in such a case to make a final coding of "ambiguous." Instances of disagreement were checked on a master code sheet, along with the final codings. The record of agreements and disagreements was used as a measure of reliability of the coding process, and the percentage of initial agreement ranged from 56/93 to 90/93. We picked 64/93 (approximately 70%) as an arbitrary reliability cutoff point, and items with lower initial agreement were omitted from subsequent analysis. (The one exception was the coding for the importance of trade, with a score of 60/93, which enters our analysis only as one variable out of 12 used to construct our scale of the relative contribution of women to subsistence—DV 10.) The reliability scores are listed along with the variables coded in appendix 3.

Two other criteria were used to eliminate items from analysis. Items for which information was available or that applied to less than 62 of our 93 cultures were also eliminated. Some items were also omitted if they showed too little variance to provide a fruitful basis for analysis, for instance an item dealing with attendance at funeral ceremonies, where only four cultures departed from the pattern of equal attendance by both sexes. In addition a number of items were included in our coding form that did not enter into our analysis because of their lack of relevance to the hypotheses under investigation. Items omitted from analysis for any of these reasons are not included in appendix 3, but a listing of them is available to interested parties on request from the author.

The primary, secondary, and reliability codes were then transferred from the master coding forms to key-punching sheets and then to computer cards. In a large number of cases the data were collapsed into fewer categories in order to permit manageable analysis. The variables discussed in chapters III and IV are the collapsed versions, although the intercoder agreement scores given for these same variables in appendix 3 refer to their original uncollapsed forms. Again, those interested may obtain copies of the original coding form and of the data before this collapsing was carried out by writing the author.

An important step in the preliminary stages of the analysis was the construction of the many scales used in this study. Some of these have been described in detail in the body of this study. The computer analysis was carried out using the MIDAS and OSIRIS computer systems accessible through the Michigan Terminal System at the University of Michigan, with programming carried out by the author with the assistance of Patricia Paul and with the advice and aid of Daniel Ayres, John Fox, and Tom Wilkinson. A special Guttman scaling program was used to construct the many scales of this type, using a program designed by Charles Cell and adapted for use on the Michigan Terminal System by Daniel Ayres. Except where other procedures have been indicated in earlier chapters, our other scales were constructed by taking equally weighted sums of the constituent items (which means dividing each item by the total number of categories in it and summing), with missing data handled by basing the sum on the remaining items.

Cross-Cultural Sample

NOTE: We include here the name of the culture as used in this study and the number of the culture as it appears in the Murdock and White sample. We also note the specific group and time to which the information refers and the names of the authors of the main sources used in our coding. In most cases these also correspond to those indicated by Murdock and White and may include additional authorities drawn from the Ethnographic Atlas published periodically in the journal *Ethnology*. Full bibliographical citations of all the sources we used can be obtained from the author upon request.

1. Nama Hottentot: The Geillkhauan tribe reconstructed for 1860.
   A. W. Hoernle, L. Schultze, and I. Shapera
3. Thonga: The Ronga subtribe around Lourenço Marques in 1895.
   H. A. Junod
5. Mbundu: The Bailundo subtribe in 1890.
   W. Hambly and G. M. Childs
7. Bemba of Zambia in 1897.
   A. I. Richards
9. Hadza in 1930.
   D. F. Bleek, J. Woodburn
11. Kikuyu of Metume or Fort Mall district in 1920.
    J. Kenyatta, L.S.B. Leakey
13. Mbuti: The epulu net-hunters of the Ituri forest in 1950.
    C. M. Turnbull
15. Banen: The Ndiki subtribe in 1935.
    I. Dugast

17. Ibo of the Isu-Ama division in 1935.
    T. Northcote, M. Green, and V. Uchendu
19. Ashanti of Kumasi state in 1895.
    R. S. Rattray, M. Fortes
21. Wolof of Upper and Lower Salum in Gambia in 1950.
    D. W. Ames, D. P. Gamble
23. Tallensi in 1934.
    M. Fortes
25. Wodaabe Fulani of Niger in 1951.
    M. Dupire, D. J. Stenning
27. Massa of Cameroon in 1910.
    I. de Garine, G. von Hagen
29. Fur around Jebel Marra in 1880.
    A. C. Beaton, R. W. Felkin
31. Shilluk in 1910.
    D. Westermann, E. E. Evans-Pritchard
33. Kaffa in 1905.
    M. Gruhl, G.W.B. Huntingford
35. Konso in the vicinity of Busc in 1935.
    C. R. Hallpike, R. Kluckhohn
37. Amhara of the Gondar district in 1953.
    S. D. Messing
39. Kenuzi Nubians in 1900.
    R. Herzog
41. Tuareg of Abaggar in 1900.
    H. Lhote, J. Nicolaisen
43. Egyptians of the town and environs of Silwa in 1950.
    H. Ammar
45. Babylonians of the city and environs of Babylon in
    1750 B.C.
    H. Suggs, G. Contenau
47. Turks of the Anatolian plateau in 1950.
    M. Makal, P. Stirling, J. E. Pierce
49. Romans of the city and environs of Rome in A.D. 110.
    J. Carcopino, L. Friedlander, M. Pellisson
51. Irish of Kinvarra parish in 1955.
    R. Cresswell, C. Arensberg

53. Yurak Samoyed in 1894.
    K. Donner, A. Engelhardt
55. Abkhaz in 1880.
    M. Dzhanashvili, L. J. Luzbetak, Ya. S. Smirnova
57. Kurds in and near the town of Rowanduz in 1951.
    E. Leach, W. Masters
59. West Punjabi of the village of Mohla in 1950.
    M. Darling, Z. Eglar
61. Toda of the Nilgiri hills in 1900.
    M. B. Emeneau, W.H.R. Rivers
63. Uttar Pradesh in and near Senapur village in 1945.
    B. S. Cohn, M. Opler, R. Singh
65. Kazak of the Great Horde in 1885.
    N. I. Grodekov, A. E. Hudson
67. Lolo of Taliang Shan mountains in 1910.
    H. M. D'Ollone, Y. Y. Lin, C. L. Tseng
69. Garo of Rengsanggri and neighboring villages in 1955.
    R. Burling, C. Nakane
71. Burmese of Nondwin village in 1960.
    M. Nash, J. G. Scott
73. North Vietnamese of the Red River delta in 1930.
    P. Gourou
75. Khmer Cambodians circa 1860.
    E. Aymonier, J. Delbert, G. Poree, and E. Maspero
77. Semang of the Jahi subtribe in 1925.
    I. Evans, P. Schebesta
79. Andamanese of the Aka Bea tribe in 1860.
    E. H. Man, A. R. Radcliffe-Brown
81. Tanala of the Menabe subtribe in 1925.
    R. Linton
83. Javanese in the vicinity of Pare in 1955.
    H. Geertz, A. Dewey, R. R. Jay
85. Iban of the Uli Ai group in 1950.
    J. D. Freeman
87. Toradja of the Bar'e subgroup in 1910.
    N. Adriani and A. C. Kruijt

89. Alorese of Atimelang in 1938.
    C. DuBois
91. Aranda of Alice Springs in 1896.
    T.G.H. Strehlow, B. Spencer, and F. J. Gillin
93. Kimam of the village of Bamol in 1960.
    L. M. Serpenti
95. Kwoma of the Hongwam subtribe in 1937.
    J.W.M. Whiting
97. New Irelanders of Lesu village in 1930.
    H. Powdermaker
99. Siuai of the northeastern group in 1939.
    D. L. Oliver
101. Pentecost Islanders of Bunlap village in 1953.
    R. B. and B. S. Lane
103. Ajie of Neje chiefdom in 1845.
    J. Guiart, M. Leenhardt
105. Marquesans circa 1860.
    E.S.C. Handy, R. Linton, R. C. Suggs
107. Gilbertese of Makin Island in 1890.
    B. Lambert
109. Trukese of Romonum Island in 1947.
    W. H. Goodenough, F. Lebar, T. Gladwin, and S. Sarason
111. Paulauans of Koror Island in 1873.
    H. G. Barnett, A. Kramer
113. Atayal in 1930.
    Y. Okada, Y. F. Rueh, C. L. Chen
115. Manchu of the Aigun district in 1915.
    S. M. Shirokogoroff
117. Japanese of southern Okayama prefecture in 1950.
    R. Beardsley, G. DeVos
119. Gilyak in 1880.
    L. Shternberg
121. Chukchee of the Reindeer group in 1900.
    W. Bogoras
123. Aleut of the Unalaska branch in 1778.
    G. Sarytschew, I. Veniaminov

125. Montagnais of the Lake St. John and Mistassini bands in 1910.
    F. Speck, J. E. Lips, J. A. Burgesse
127. Salteaux of the Berens River, Little Grand Rapids, and Pekangekum Bands in 1930.
    A. I. Hallowell, A. Skinner
129. Kaska of the Upper Liard River in 1900.
    J. J. Honigmann
131. Haida of the village of Masset in 1875.
    J. R. Swanton, G. P. Murdock
133. Twana in 1860.
    M. Eells, W. W. Elmendorf
135. Eastern Pomo of Clear Lake in 1850.
    S. A. Barrett, E. W. Gifford, E. M. Loeb
137. Wadadika Paitute of Harney Valley in 1870.
    F. A. Riddell, B. B. Whiting
139. Kutenai of the Lower or Eastern branch in 1890.
    A. F. Chamberlain, H. H. Turney-High
141. Hidatsa of Hidatsa village in 1836.
    A. W. Bowers, W. Matthews
143. Omaha in 1860.
    J. W. Dorsey, A. Fletcher, and F. LaFlesche
145. Creek of the Upper Creek division in 1800.
    J. R. Swanton
147. Comanche in 1970.
    E. A. Hoebel
149. Zuni in 1880.
    F. H. Cushing, M. C. Stevenson
151. Papago of the Archie division in 1910.
    R. Underhill
153. Aztec of the city and environs of Tenochtitlan in 1520.
    F. B. de Sahagun, J. Soustelle, G. C. Vaillant
155. Quiche of the town of Chichicastenango in 1930.
    R. Bunzel, L. S. Schultze-Jena
157. Bribri tribe of Talamanca in 1917.
    A. Skinner, D. Stone

159. Goajiro in 1947.
    G. Bolinder, V. G. de Pineda
161. Callinago of Dominica in 1650.
    R. Breton, D. Taylor
163. Yanomamo of the Shamatri tribe in 1965.
    N. A. Chagnon
165. Saramacca of the upper Suriname River in 1928.
    A. M. Coster, M. C. Khan, M. J. and F. S. Herskovitz
167. Cubeo of the Caduiaria River in 1939.
    I. Goldman
169. Jivaro in 1920.
    R. Karsten, M. W. Stirling
171. Inca in the vicinity of Cuzco in 1530.
    P. de C. de Leon, B. Cobo, R. Rowe
173. Siriono near the Rio Blanco in 1942.
    A. Holmberg
175. Trumai in 1938.
    R. Murphy and B. Quain
177. Tupinamba in the vicinity of Rio de Janiero in 1550.
    A. Thevet, A. Metraux
179. Shavante in the vicinity of São Domingo in 1958.
    D. Maybury-Lewis
181. Cayua of southern Mato Grosso in 1890.
    J. B. Watson, V. D. Watson
183. Abipon in 1750.
    M. Dobrizhoffer
185. Tehuelche in 1870.
    G. C. Musters

Variables Used in this Study

NOTE: Included here are the names and numbers of all the variables used in our analysis. When appropriate we also include the intercoder agreement score (ICA) for each variable. These refer to initial agreements between coders for the uncollapsed versions of the codes, rather than for the collapsed versions actually used in computations. Finally, the page where each variable is first introduced in the text is noted. The actual coding form instructions, detailed category wording, procedure in collapsing coding categories, and actual scores of these variables for all of our 93 cultures are available to interested scholars upon request. The collapsed scores for DV 1-52 and DVS 1-9 are published separately in Whyte, 1978a.

DEPENDENT VARIABLES

DV 1: Sex of gods and spirits. ICA = 84%. p. 50.
DV 2: Sex of mythical founders. ICA = 78%. p. 51.
DV 3: Sex of shamans. ICA = 85%. p. 52.
DV 4: Sex of reputed witches. ICA = 85%. pp. 52-53.
DV 5: Participation by sex in religious ceremonies. ICA = 81%. p. 55.
DV 6: Funeral elaborateness by sex. ICA = 85%. p. 55.
DV 7: Sex of intermediate or local political leaders. ICA = 94%. p. 57.
DV 8: Sex of leaders of kin groups and/or extended families. ICA = 87%. p. 57.
DV 9: Participation in warfare by sex. ICA = 93%. p. 58.
DV 10: Proportional contribution of women to subsistence. A scale composed of 12 items whose ICAs range from 65% to 96%. p. 60.

DV 11: Effort on subsistence activities, by sex. ICA = 73%. pp. 62-63.

DV 12: Communitywide male work groups. ICA = 91%. p. 63.

DV 13: Communitywide female work groups. ICA = 90%. p. 63.

DV 14: Lack of sexual segregation in work. IVA = 73%. p. 64.

DV 15: Inheritance of property by sex. ICA = 73%. p. 65.

DV 16: Dwelling ownership by sex. ICA = 73%. p. 66.

DV 17: Control over fruits of male labor. ICA = 73%. p. 66.

DV 18: Control over fruits of joint labor. ICA = 77%. p. 67.

DV 19: Control over fruits of female labor. ICA = 74%. p. 67.

DV 20: Division of domestic work. ICA = 80%. p. 68.

DV 21: Lack of a premarital sexual double standard. ICA = 81%. p. 69.

DV 22: Lack of an extramarital sexual double standard. ICA = 75%. p. 69.

DV 23: Sexual affairs by women. ICA = 73%. p. 69.

DV 24: Menstrual taboos. A 7-point Guttman scale. pp. 70-71.

DV 25: View of procreation. ICA = 84%. pp. 71-72.

DV 26: View of sex drives. ICA = 86%. p. 72.

DV 27: Absence of danger from sexual activity. ICA = 91%. p. 73.

DV 28: Voice of elders in marriage. ICA = 69%. p. 74.

DV 29: Voice of couple in marriage. ICA = 74%. p. 74.

DV 30: Marriage finance. ICA = 75%. p. 75.

DV 31: Marriage forms. ICA = 81%. p. 75.

DV 32: Multiple spouses allowed. ICA = 97%. p. 76.

DV 33: Absence of levirate. ICA = 89%. p. 76.

DV 34: Distance of moves at marriage. ICA = 95%. p. 77.

DV 35: Relative ease of divorce. ICA = 85%. pp. 77-78.

DV 36: Relative ease of remarriage. ICA = 84%. p. 78.

DV 37: Relative ages at first marriage. ICA = 97%. p. 79.

DV 38: Final authority over infants. ICA = 73%. p. 80.

DV 39: Final authority over children. ICA = 69%. p. 80.

DV 40: Wife to husband deference. A 5-point Guttman scale. p. 81.

DV 41: Child preference. ICA = 89%. p. 82.

DV 42: Infanticide. ICA = 96%. p. 82.

DV 43: Relative age of training for adult duties. ICA = 87% p. 83.

DV 44: Relative punishment of children. ICA = 88%. p. 83.

DV 45: Physical punishment of spouse. ICA = 95%. p. 84.

DV 46: Lack of general husband dominance. ICA = 88%. p. 84.

DV 47: Relative participation in community gatherings. ICA = 86%. p. 85.

DV 48: Female initiation ceremonies. A 5-point Guttman scale. p. 86.

DV 49: Belief in change in women's status. ICA = 94%. p. 87.

DV 50: Lack of machismo concerns. ICA = 74%. p. 87.

DV 51: Lack of a belief in female inferiority. ICA = 84%. p. 88.

DV 52: Women's informal influence. A 3-point scale. ICA = 84%. p. 88.

DVS 1: Property control scale. A 4-point scale. p. 98. (Composed of DV 15, DV 16, DV 17, DV18, and DV 19)

DVS 2: Kin power scale. A 3-point scale. p. 98. (Composed of DV 8, DV 31, DV 32, and DV 33)

DVS 3: Value of life scale. A 3-point scale, p. 99. (Composed of DV 41, DV 42, and DV 45)

DVS 4: Value of labor scale. A 5-point scale, p.99. (Composed of DV 10, DV 11, and DV 30 reversed)

DVS 5: Domestic authority scale. A 4-point scale. p. 99. (Composed of DV 38, DV 39, and DV 46)

DVS 6: Ritualized female solidarity scale. A 3-point scale. p. 99. (Composed of DV 12, DV 13, DV 24, DV 48, and DV 51)

DVS 7: Control of sex scale. A 3-point scale. pp. 99-100. (Composed of DV 21, DV 22, DV 36, and DV 37)

DVS 8: Ritualized fear scale. A 3-point scale, p. 100. (Composed of DV 6, DV 27, and DV 50)

DVS 9: Joint participation scale. A 3-point scale. p. 100. (Composed of DV 9, DV 14, and DV 47)

INDEPENDENT VARIABLES

IV 1: Use of plow. ICA = 97%. p. 29.

IV 2: Use of irrigation. ICA = 93%. p. 29.

IV 3: Grain crops. ICA = 95%. p. 29.

IV 4: Root and tuber crops. ICA = 92%. p. 29.

IV 5: Tree crops. ICA = 94%. p. 29.

IV 6: Importance of agriculture. ICA = 89%. p. 29.

IV 7: Large nonmilked domestic animals. ICA = 92%. p. 30.

IV 8: Large milked domestic animals. ICA = 94%. p. 30.
IV 9: Small domestic animals. ICA = 92%. p. 30.
IV 10: Large new domestic animals. ICA = 99%. p. 30.
IV 11: Small new domestic animals. ICA = 97%. p. 30.
IV 12: Importance of herding. ICA = 79%. p. 30.
IV 13: Large animals hunted. ICA = 89%. p. 30.
IV 14: Small animals hunted. ICA = 95%. p. 30.
IV 15: Medium animals hunted. ICA = 89%. p. 31.
IV 16: Importance of hunting and gathering. ICA = 71%. p. 31.
IV 17: Frequency of intercommunity warfare. ICA = 87%. p. 32.
IV 18: Male initiation ceremonies. A 5-point Guttman scale. p. 33.
IV 19: Male solidarity. A 5-point Guttman scale, p. 33.
IV 20: Descent. ICA = 89%. p. 34.
IV 21: Postmarital residence. ICA = 92%. p. 34.
IV 22: Preferred family form. ICA = 76%. p. 36.
IV 23: Political organization. ICA = 80%. p. 37.
IV 24: Crimes punished. ICA = 92%. p. 37.
IV 25: Government bureaucrats. ICA = 94%. p. 37.
IV 26: Present kingdom. ICA = 95%. p. 37.
IV 27: Past kingdom. ICA = 98%. p. 37.
IV 28: Existence of private property. p. 38.
IV 29: Settlement type. ICA = 82%. p. 40.
IV 30: Metalworking. ICA = 90%. p. 40.
IV 31: Pottery making. ICA = 95%. p. 40.
IV 32: Weaving. ICA = 94%. p. 40.
IV 33: Social stratification in larger society. ICA = 91%. p. 40.
IV 34: Social stratification in local community. ICA = 90%. p. 40.
IV 35: Societal complexity. A 7-point Guttman scale. p. 40.

IV 36:   Type of religion. ICA = 97%. p. 42.

IV 37:   Institutionalized envy. A 4-item scale. p. 43.

IV 38:   Sex ratio. ICA = 96%. p. 44.

IV 39:   Systematic absences of males. ICA = 88%. p. 44.

IV 40 = DV 15; IV 41 = DV 13; IV 42 = DV 10; IV 43 = DV 17; IV 44 = DV 18; IV 45 = DV 19; IV 46 = DV 31.

CONTROL VARIABLES

CV 1:   Sex of coders. p. 47.

CV 2:   Number of sources consulted. p. 47.

CV 3:   Number of different authorities consulted. p. 47.

CV 4:   Total number of pages in sources consulted. p. 47.

CV 5:   Sex of authorities. p. 47.

CV 6:   Nationality of authorities. p. 47.

CV 7:   Occupation of authorities. p. 47.

CV 8:   Fieldwork training of authorities. p. 48.

CV 9:   Knowledge of native language. p. 48.

CV 10:   Total length of fieldwork. p. 48.

CV 11:   Anthropological present. p. 48 .

CV 12:   Region of the world (from Murdock and White, 1969). p. 48.

Description of the Sample

BELOW we use selected variables to describe t͟
our 93-culture sample. Given the utility of the c͟r͟
method for addressing questions of social evolutio͟
ticularly focus on those variables that differentiate t͟h͟
into small, simple, preliterate cultures and large, c͟
literate cultures. As discussed in the text, the aim of ͟
sample is to represent the full range of known, preind͟u͟
cultures as accurately as possible. Where appropriate w͟
clude the variable notation from appendix 3, although in s͟
cases the categories used in the analysis have been collap͟s͟
or expanded to provide the reader with more useful inform͟
tion.

Use of the plow (IV 1)

Yes	No	No information	Total
25	67	1	93

Use of irrigation (IV 2)

Yes	No	No information	Total
31	55	7	93

Grain crops primary? (IV 3)

Yes	No	No information	Total
47	45	1	93

Importance of agriculture to subsistence (IV 6, collapsed)

Principal or co-dominant subsistence activity	Present, but not a major subsistence activity	Insignificant	Total
64	7	22	93

Importance of hunting and gathering to subsistence
(IV 16, collapsed)

Principal or co-dominant subsistence activity	Present, but not a major subsistence activity	Insignificant	Total
26	52	15	93

Descent (IV 20, expanded)

Patrilineal	Bilateral or dual	Matrilineal	Total
44	31	18	93

Postmarital residence (IV 21, expanded)

Patri- local	Matri- patri- local	Bilocal or neolocal	Avuncu- local	Matri- local	No in- formation	Total
56	4	9	3	18	3	93

Political organization (IV 23, reduced)

Absence of local political integration	Autono- mous local community	Small state (1,500- 100,000 population)	State (100,000+)	No infor- mation	Total
11	40	13	27	2	93

Present or past kingdom (defined as a political unit with centralized organs of political control, power to tax, and rule concentrated in a single, hereditary office) (IV 26-27)

Yes	No	No information	Total
30	52	11	93

Private property recognized in property of productive value? (IV 28)

Yes	No	No information	Total
70	14	9	93

Type of settlement (IV 29)

Fully nomadic	Semi-nomadic	Dispersed homesteads or hamlets	Compact, permanent village	Larger settle-ment	No infor-mation	Total
7	21	22	28	12	3	93

Social stratification in the larger society (IV 33)

Largely absent	Differences in resources, but no distinct classes	Dual stratifica-cation, elites and commoners	Complex stratifica-cation, three or more classes	No infor-mation	Total
24	31	11	26	1	93

Societal complexity (IV 35, reduced)

None of the latter present	+Crimes punished by gov-ernment	+Specialized priests, formal edu-cation, or written lan-guage present	+Full time bureaucrats unrelated to gov't. head	Total
37	13	18	25	93

Type of religion (IV 36)

Classical (Christianity, Islam, Buddhism, Hinduism)	Mixed classical and pre-classical	Pre-classical	Total
14	31	48	93

Symbolic medium of exchange—money—present?

Yes	No	No information	Total
59	32	2	93

Written language—present?

Yes	No	No information	Total
31	59	3	93

206

Anthropological present (CV 11)

Prior to 1800	1800– 1900	1901– 1950	1950– present	Total
8	34	40	11	93

Region of the world (CV 12)

Sub-Saharan Africa	Circum-Mediterranean	East Eurasia	Insular Pacific	North America	South America	Total
13	15	17	16	16	16	93

Bibliography

Aberle, David, 1961. "Matrilineal Descent in Cross-Cultural Perspective." In David Schneider and Kathleen Gough, eds., *Matrilineal Kinship*, Berkeley: University of California Press.

Andreski, Stanislav, 1968. *Military Organization and Society*, 2nd ed., Berkeley: University of California Press.

Bachofen, J. J., 1861. *Das Mutterrecht*, Stuttgart: Kraus & Hoffman.

Bamberger, Joan, 1974. "The Myth of Matriarchy: Why Men Rule in Primitive Society." In M. Z. Rosaldo and L. Lamphere, eds., *Woman, Culture, and Society*, Stanford: Stanford University Press.

Bardis, Panos, 1963. "Synopsis and Evaluation of Theories Concerning Family Evolution," *Social Science*, vol. 38, no. 50, January.

Barry, Herbert, III; Bacon, Margaret K.; and Child, Irvin L., 1957. "A Cross-Cultural Survey of Some Sex Differences in Socialization," *Journal of Abnormal and Social Psychology* 55; 327-332.

Bettelheim, Bruno, 1954. *Symbolic Wounds*, New York: Free Press.

Blake, Judith, 1974. "The Changing Status of Women in Developed Countries," *Scientific American*, vol. 231, September.

Blood, Robert O., Jr., and Wolfe, Donald M., 1960. *Husbands and Wives*, New York: Free Press.

Blumberg, Rae L., and Winch, Robert F., 1972. "Societal Complexity and Familial Complexity: Evidence for the Curvilinear Hypothesis," *American Journal of Sociology*, vol. 77, no. 5.

Boserup, Ester, 1970. *Woman's Role in Economic Development*, New York: St. Martin's Press.

Brown, Judith K., 1963. "A Cross-Cultural Study of Female Initiation Rites," *American Anthropologist* 65: 837-853.

Brown, Judith K., 1970. "Economic Organization and the Position of Women among the Iroquois," *Ethnohistory*, vol. 17, nos. 3-4.

Burling, Robbins, 1963. *Rengsanggri*, Philadelphia: University of Pennsylvania Press.

Choudhury, B., 1958. *Some Cultural and Linguistic Aspects of the Garos*, Guahati: Lawyer's Book Stall.

Clignet, Remi, 1970. *Many Wives, Many Powers*, Evanston: Northwestern University Press.

Coale, Ansley J., 1965. "Estimates of Average Size of Household." In A. J. Coale et al., eds., *Aspects of the Analysis of Family Structure*, Princeton: Princeton University Press.

Coleman, James S., 1971. *Resources for Social Change*, New York: John Wiley & Sons.

Collins, Randall, 1971. "A Conflict Theory of Sexual Stratification," *Social Problems*, vol. 19, no. 1.

D'Andrade, Roy G., 1966. "Sex Differences and Cultural Institutions." In Eleanor Maccoby, ed., *The Development of Sex Differences*, Stanford: Stanford University Press.

Davis, Elizabeth Gould, 1971. *The First Sex*, New York: G. P. Putnam's Sons.

De Beauvoir, Simone, 1949. *The Second Sex*, Harmondsworth, England: Penguin Books (1972 edition).

Devereux, George, 1950. "The Psychology of Feminine Genital Bleeding," *International Journal of Psychoanalysis* 31: 237-257.

Eells, M., 1877. "Twana Indians of Skokomish Reservation in Washington Territory," Bulletin of the U.S. Geological and Geographical Survey of the Territories, vol. 3.

Ehrenfels, O. R., 1947. *Mother-Right in India*, Myderabad: Government Central Press.

Elmendorf, W. W., 1948. "The Cultural Setting of the Twana Secret Society," *American Anthropologist*, vol. 50.

Elmendorf, W. W., 1960. "The Structures of Twana Culture," Washington State University Research Studies, vol. 2.

Ember, Melvin, and Ember, Carol R., 1971. "The Conditions Favoring Matrilocal versus Patrilocal Residence," *American Anthropologist,* vol. 73, no. 3.

210

Engels, Friedrich, 1902. *The Origins of the Family, Private Property and the State*, Chicago: Charles H. Kerr.

Evans-Pritchard, E. E., 1965. *The Position of Women in Primitive Societies and Other Essays in Social Anthropology*, New York: Free Press.

Ferris, Abbott L., 1971. *Indicators of Trends in the Status of American Women*, New York: Russell Sage Foundation.

Ford, Clellan S., and Beach, Frank A., 1951. *Patterns of Sexual Behavior*, New York: Harper & Row.

Friedl, Ernestine, 1975. *Women and Men*, New York: Holt, Rinehart, and Winston.

Goldberg, Steven, 1973. *The Inevitability of Patriarchy*, New York: William Morrow & Co.

Goodale, Jane C., 1971. *Tiwi Wives*, Seattle: University of Washington Press.

Goldschmidt, W., and Kunkel, E. J., 1971. "The Structure of the Peasant Family," *American Anthropologist* 73: 1058-1076.

Goode, William J., 1963. *World Revolution and Family Patterns*, New York: Free Press.

Goodman, Leo A., and Kruskal, William H., 1954. "Measures of Association for Cross-Classifications," *Journal of the American Statistical Association*, vol. 49, December.

Goody, Jack, 1969. "Inheritance, Property, and Marriage in Africa and Eurasia," *Sociology* 3, no. 1: 55-76.

Goody, Jack, 1973. "Bridewealth and Dowry in Africa and Eurasia." In J. Goody and S. J. Tambiah, *Bridewealth and Dowry*, Cambridge, Eng.: Cambridge University Press.

Gough, Kathleen, 1972. "An Anthropologist Looks at Engels." In Nona Glazer-Malbin and Helen Youngelson Waehrer, eds., *Woman in a Man-Made World*, Chicago: Rand McNally & Co.

Gouldner, Alvin W., and Peterson, Richard A., 1962. *Notes on Technology and the Moral Order*, Indianapolis: Bobbs-Merrill Co.

Harris, Marvin, 1974. *Cows, Pigs, Wars and Witches*, New York: Vintage Press.

Hays, H. R. 1964. *The Dangerous Sex*, New York: G. P. Putnam's Sons.

Hays, William L., 1963. *Statistics for Psychologists*, New York: Holt, Rinehart, and Winston.

211

Heath, D. B., 1958. "Sexual Division of Labor and Cross-Cultural Research," *Social Forces* 37: 77-79.

Hobhouse, L. T., 1924. *Morals in Evolution*, London: Chapman and Hall.

Hobhouse, L. T.; Wheeler, G. C., and Ginsberg, M., 1915. *The Material Culture and Social Institutions of the Simpler Peoples*, London: Chapman and Hall.

Holter, Harriet, 1970. *Sex Roles and Social Structure*, Oslo: Universitetsforlaget.

Jackson, Elton, 1962. "Status Consistency and Symptoms of Stress," *American Sociological Review* 27: 469-480.

Lebeuf, Annie M. D., 1963. "The Role of Women in the Political Organization of African Societies." In Denise Paulme, ed., *Women of Tropical Africa*, Berkeley: University of California Press.

Lenski, Gerhard, 1954. "Status Crystallization: A Non-Vertical Dimension of Social Status," *American Sociological Review* 19: 405-413.

Lenski, Gerhard, 1970. *Human Societies*, New York: McGraw-Hill.

Levine, Robert A., 1966. "Sex Roles and Economic Change in Africa," *Ethnology*, vol. 5, no. 2.

Lowie, Robert H., 1920. *Primitive Society*, New York: Liveright.

Marsh, Robert M., 1967. *Comparative Sociology*, New York: Harcourt, Brace and World.

Mead, Margaret, 1949. *Male and Female*, New York: William Morrow and Co.

Mead, Margaret, 1971. "Why We Fear Witches," *Redbook*, vol. 138, no. 1, November.

Mellaart, James H., 1967. *Catal Huyuk*, New York: McGraw-Hill.

Mencher, Joan, 1965. "The Nayars of South Malabar." In M. F. Nimkoff, ed., *Comparative Family Systems*, Boston: Houghton Mifflin Co.

Michaelson, E. A., and Goldschmidt, W., 1971. "Female Roles and Male Dominance among Peasants," *Southwestern Journal of Anthropology* 27: 330-352.

Millett, Kate, 1969. *Sexual Politics*, London: Abacus (1972 edition).

212

Minturn, Leigh, and Lambert, William W., 1964. *Mothers of Six Cultures*, New York: John Wiley & Sons.

Minturn, Leigh; Grosse, Martin; and Haider, Santoah; "Cultural Patterning of Sexual Beliefs and Behavior," *Ethnology*, vol. 5.

Montagu, Ashley, 1968. *The Natural Superiority of Women*, New York: Macmillan Co., rev. ed.

Morgan, Elaine, 1972. *The Descent of Woman*, New York: Stein & Day.

Morgan, Louis Henry, 1877. *Ancient Society*, London: Macmillan & Co.

Murdock, G. P., 1937. "Comparative Data on Division of Labor by Sex," *Social Forces* 15: 551-553.

Murdock, G. P., 1949. *Social Structure*, New York: Macmillan Co.

Murdock, G. P., 1950. "Family Stability in Non-European Cultures," *Annals of the American Academy of Political and Social Science* 272: 195-201.

Murdock, G. P., 1957. "Anthropology as a Comparative Science," *Behavioral Science* 2: 249-254.

Murdock, G. P., 1961. "World Ethnographic Sample." In Frank W. Moore, ed., *Readings in Cross-Cultural Methodology*, New Haven: Human Relations Area Files Press.

Murdock, G. P., 1968. "World Sampling Provinces," *Ethnology*, 7: 304-326.

Murdock, G. P., and White, D. R., 1969. "Standard Cross-Cultural Sample," *Ethnology* 8: 329-369.

Nakane, Chie, 1967. *Garo and Khasi: A Comparative Study in Matrilineal Kin Groups*, The Hague: Mouton.

Naroll, Raoul, 1962. *Data Quality Control*, New York: Free Press.

Naroll, Raoul, 1970a. "Cross-Cultural Sampling." In Raoul Naroll and Ronald Cohen, eds., *A Handbook of Method in Cultural Anthropology*, Garden City: Natural History Press.

Naroll, Raoul, 1970b. "Galton's Problem," in ibid.

Nimkoff, M. F., 1965. *Comparative Family Systems*, Boston: Houghton Mifflin Co.

Nimkoff, M. F., and Middleton, Russell, 1960. "Types of Family and Types of Economy," *American Journal of Sociology* 66: 215-225.

213

O'Leary, Timothy J., 1970. "Ethnographic Bibliographies." In Raoul Naroll and Ronald Cohen, eds., *A Handbook of Method in Cultural Anthropology*, Garden City: Natural History Press.

Osmond, Marie W., 1964. "Toward Monogamy," master's thesis, Florida State University. Cited in M. F. Nimkoff, *Comparative Family Systems*, Boston: Houghton Mifflin Co.

Osmond, Marie W., 1969. "A Cross-Cultural Analysis of Family Organization," *Journal of Marriage and the Family* 31: 302-310.

Paige, Karen E., 1973. "Women Learn to Sing the Menstrual Blues," *Psychology Today*, vol. 7, no. 4.

Parish, William L., Jr., and Whyte, Martin King, 1978. *Village and Family in Contemporary China*, Chicago: University of Chicago Press.

Ruether, Rosemary R., ed., 1974. *Religion and Sexism*, New York: Simon & Schuster.

Sacks, Karen, 1971. "Comparative Notes on the Position of Women." Paper delivered at the annual meetings of the American Anthropological Association.

Sacks, Karen, 1974. "Engels Revisited: Women, the Organization of Production, and Private Property." In M. Z. Rosaldo and L. Lamphere, eds., *Woman, Culture and Society*, Stanford: Stanford University Press.

Sacks, Michael P., 1974. "Sex Roles in Soviet Russia," Ph.D. dissertation, University of Michigan.

Sanday, Peggy, R., 1973. "Toward a Theory of the Status of Women," *American Anthropologist* 75: 1682-1700.

Sanday, Peggy R., 1974. "Female Status in the Public Domain." In M. Z. Rosaldo and L. Lamphere, op. cit.

Schlegel, Alice, 1972. *Male Dominance and Female Autonomy*, New Haven: Human Relations Area Files Press.

Scott, Joan W., and Tilly, Louis A., 1975. "Women's Work and Family in Nineteenth Century Europe," *Comparative Studies in Society and History* 17, no. 1: 36-64.

Simmons, Leo W., 1945. *The Role of the Aged in Primitive Society*, New Haven: Yale University Press.

Stephens, William N., 1962. *The Oedipus Complex: Cross-Cultural Evidence*, New York: Free Press.

214

Stephens, William N., 1963. *The Family in Cross-Cultural Perspective*, New York: Holt, Rinehart, and Winston.

Steward, Julian, 1955. *Theory of Culture Change*, Urbana: University of Illinois Press.

Tambiah, S. J., 1973. "Dowry and Bridewealth and the Property Rights of Women in South Asia." In J. Goody and S. J. Tambiah, *Bridewealth and Dowry*, Cambridge, Eng.: Cambridge University Press.

Textor, Robert B., 1967. *A Cross-Cultural Summary*, New Haven: Human Relations Area Files Press.

Tiger, Lionel, 1969. *Men in Groups*, New York: Random House.

Wallace, Anthony F. C., 1971. "Handsome Lake and the Decline of the Iroquois Matriarchate." In Francis L. K. Hsu, ed., *Kinship and Culture*, Chicago: Aldine.

Wallace, David L., 1968. "Clustering." In *The International Encyclopedia of the Social Sciences*, New York: Crowell Collier.

Whiting, B., ed., 1963. *Six Cultures*, New York: John Wiley & Sons.

Whyte, Martin King, 1978a. "Cross-Cultural Codes Dealing with the Relative Status of Women," *Ethnology*, forthcoming.

Whyte, Martin King, 1978b. "Cross-Cultural Studies of Women and the Male Bias Problem," *Behavior Science Research*, forthcoming.

Wolf, Margery, 1972. *Women and the Family in Rural Taiwan*, Stanford: Stanford University Press.

Young, Frank W., 1965. *Initiation Ceremonies*, Indianapolis: Bobbs-Merrill Co.

Young, Frank W., and Bacdayan, A. A., 1965. "Menstrual Taboos and Social Rigidity," *Ethnology*, vol. 4, no. 2, April.

Zelman, Elizabeth A. C., 1974. "Women's Rights and Women's Rites: A Cross-Cultural Study of Womanpower and Reproductive Ritual," Ph.D. dissertation, University of Michigan.

215

Index

Aberle, David, 156
Africa, status of women in, 157, 161-62
agrarian societies, *see* intensive agriculture
America, status of women in, 174
animal herding, 28-30, 201-202; and the status of women, 126-27
anthropological present, 17, 20-21, 48, 186, 207
Ayres, Daniel, 191

Bachofen, J. J., 8
Barry, Herbert, 9, 187
Bettelheim, Bruno, 42
birth ceremonies, 56
Blake, Judith, 182n
Blumberg, Rae L. and Robert F. Winch, 39, 141n
Boserup, Ester, 44, 48
bride price, *see* marriage finance
Brown, Judith K., 9, 44, 59-62
Bunzel, Ruth, 23n
Burling, Robbins, 111

Catal Huyuk, 8
Cell, Charles, 191
cereal grains, *see* intensive agriculture
childcare burdens, 27n, 28, 68, 179
child preference, 82-83, 200. *See also* value of life scale
children, authority over, 80-81, 200. *See also* domestical authority scale

child training, 83-84, 200
China, status of women in, 175
chi-square statistic, 121
classical religions, *see* religion practiced
Clignet, Remi, 45
cluster analysis, 97-98
Coale, Ansley, 135
Collins, Randall, 3, 36
community participation, 85, 200. *See also* joint participation scale
complex societies, *see* societal complexity
control of sex scale, 99-100, 118, 158-61, 201
cross-cultural sample: explained, 5, 13ff; listed 192-97
cross-cultural survey: coding procedures, 24-25, 187ff; defined, 5, 13, 16, 173
cross-national survey, 13, 16, 173, 175
culture: defined, 13; distinguished from society, 13

Davis, Elizabeth Gould, 8, 51
de Beauvoir, Simone, 178-79
deference toward husbands, 81-82, 200
dependent variables, 44; and the status of women, 145-47; defined, 28; listed, 198-200; scales, 98-100, 201
differentiation, *see* societal complexity

217

INDEX

house ownership, *see* dwelling
ownership
housework, *see* domestic work
Human Relations Area Files, 14,
186, 188
hunting and gathering societies,
5, 16, 20, 28, 30-31, 202, 205;
and the status of women, 126-
29, 162n, 171, 189

independent variables, 44; defined, 27-28; listed, 200-203
industrial societies and the status
of women, 19-20, 173, 181-84
infanticide, 82, 200. *See also*
value of life scale
informal influence of women,
22-23, 88, 104, 119, 135, 200
inheritance rights, *see* property,
control over
initiation ceremonies: for females, 86, 200; for males, 33,
202. *See also* female solidarity; male solidarity
intensive agriculture, 28-30, 40,
201, 204; and the status of
women, 124-26, 139, 157-66,
183-84. *See also* societal complexity
inter-coder agreement scores, *see*
reliability of data

Jackson, Elton, 176
Java, status of women in, 91n
joint participation scale, 100,
102, 105, 119, 159-62, 201

kingdoms, *see* political organization
kin power scale, 98, 118, 201
kinship group leaders, 57-58,
198. *See also* kin power scale

Lebeuf, Annie, 57
Lenski, Gerhard, 17, 38, 153, 176

Levine, Robert A., 42, 107-108n
levirate, 76-77, 200. *See also* kin
power scale
Lowie, Robert H., 89, 95, 104,
107, 119, 168

machismo, 87, 200. *See also* ritualized fear scale
male absence, 31-32, 43-44, 143-
44, 203
male bias, in anthropological
research, 22, 148-50; in religious doctrines, 41
male bonding, *see* Tiger, L.
male dominance, 84, 90-94, 200.
See also domestic authority
scale
male solidarity, 32-33, 63, 165n,
199, 202; and the status of
women, 131-32
male strength, *see* animal herding; hunting and gathering;
intensive agriculture; warfare
marriage decisions, voice of men
and women in, 74-75, 199
marriage finance, 75, 100-101,
183, 199; and societal complexity, 157-62. *See also* value of
labor scale
marriage, relative ages at, 79-80,
102, 200. *See also* control of
sex scale
marriage rules, 44, 46, 73, 75-76,
158, 160-62, 199; and the
status of women, 145-47,
165n. *See also* kin power scale
Marsh, Robert M., 17, 38, 153
Marxist theory, *see* Engels,
Friedrich
matriarchy, 6-7, 86-87, 164
matrilineal descent, 7, 33-34,
202, 205; and societal complexity, 156; and the status of
women, 132-34, 156, 165-66n,
171

219

LIBRARY OF CONGRESS CATALOGING IN PUBLICATION DATA
Whyte, Martin King.
  The status of women in preindustrial societies.

  Bibliography: p.
  Includes index.
  1. Women—Social conditions.   2. Sex role.
3. Cross-cultural studies.   I. Title.
GN479.7.W48   301.41'2   77-85574
  ISBN 0-691-09380-6